PRAISE FOR THE COOKBOOKS OF CLAIRE CRISCUOLO:

Claire's Corner Copia Cookbook

"A down-home vegetarian classic."
—*Miami Herald*

"If you're looking for fresh ideas, you'll find them in this book."
—*Vegetarian Times*

"The recipes are remarkably quick, fresh, and tasty . . . Cooks will appreciate the depth of flavor achieved with minimal effort."
—*Portland Oregonian*

Claire's Classic American Vegetarian Cooking

"Savory . . . even if you're not a vegetarian, you may want to include these veggie meals in your diet." —*Philadelphia Forum*

"Provides a chance to convert the carnivores at your dinner table."
—*Denver Post*

"Offers interesting vegetarian alternatives to traditional meat-based dishes."
—*Evansville News*

CLAIRE CRISCUOLO is the author of *Claire's Corner Copia Cookbook* (Plume, 1994) and *Claire's Classic American Vegetarian Cooking: 225 New and Favorite Homestyle Vegetarian Recipes*. She is the chef and owner of Claire's Corner Copia in New Haven, Connecticut, one of the nation's oldest and most popular vegetarian restaurants, which she founded with her husband in 1975. Claire teaches cooking classes nationwide, promoting the benefits and pleasures of vegetarian cooking.

Claire's Italian Feast

165 VEGETARIAN RECIPES
FROM NONNA'S KITCHEN

Claire Criscuolo

A PLUME BOOK

PLUME
Published by the Penguin Group
Penguin Putnam Inc., 375 Hudson Street, New York, New York 10014, U.S.A.
Penguin Books Ltd, 27 Wrights Lane, London W8 5TZ, England
Penguin Books Australia Ltd, Ringwood, Victoria, Australia
Penguin Books Canada Ltd, 10 Alcorn Avenue, Toronto, Ontario, Canada M4V 3B2
Penguin Books (N.Z.) Ltd, 182–190 Wairau Road, Auckland 10, New Zealand

Penguin Books Ltd, Registered Offices: Harmondsworth, Middlesex, England

First published by Plume, an imprint of Dutton NAL, a member of Penguin Putnam Inc.

First Printing, October, 1998
10   9   8   7   6   5   4   3   2   1

Ⓟ REGISTERED TRADEMARK—MARCA REGISTRADA

LIBRARY OF CONGRESS CATALOGING-IN-PUBLICATION DATA:
Criscuolo, Claire.
[Italian feast]
Claire's Italian feast : 165 vegetarian recipes from Nonna's kitchen / Claire Criscuolo.
p.   cm.
Includes index.
ISBN 0-452-27881-3
1. Vegetarian cookery.   2. Cookery, Italian—Southern style.
I. Title.
TX837.C77224   1998
641.5'636—dc21   98-25758
                                                       CIP

Printed in the United States of America
Set in Adobe Garamond and Zirkon
Designed by Eve L. Kirch

BOOKS ARE AVAILABLE AT QUANTITY DISCOUNTS WHEN USED TO PROMOTE PRODUCTS OR SERVICES. FOR INFORMATION PLEASE WRITE TO PREMIUM MARKETING DIVISION, PENGUIN PUTNAM INC., 375 HUDSON STREET, NEW YORK, NEW YORK 10014.

This book is dedicated with tremendous love to my grandmother,
Assunta Maria Lucibello Bigio,
and to my mother, Anna Pasqualina Bigio LaPia Cassella,
two women who taught me the great importance of an Italian kitchen
and the love that radiates from the heart of the home.

Acknowledgments

$\mathcal{I}$ am firmly convinced that no one reaches a goal without support from others, and this book is a testament to that.

Since I was a little girl, I have been truly blessed with a loving family and great friends who are both kind and generous, and I value them more than words can say.

Claire's Corner Copia, my beloved twenty-three-year-old vegetarian restaurant, is the reason that I started writing cookbooks. Claire's could have never become and remained the huge success that it is without the help of so many wonderful people. My husband, Frank, and I will always be grateful to our families, who continue to provide support and guidance—my mom continues to cook at Claire's. I am especially thankful to Donald Jackson (I call him my Rock of Gibraltar), Rose Albin, Mike Pacileo (our dedicated general manager), Thimika Vega, Bill Molta, Margarita Hernandez, Donna Izzo, and the many caring employees who have contributed to our success. After all, a business is only as good as its staff! And over the years I have been blessed with a highly talented staff, to whom I will always be grateful.

Our customers give us the reasons to cook and clean and shop—and to smile. Thank you. Special thanks to our vendors, our repair and maintenance crew, and to our city for keeping our neighborhood across from Yale University so beautiful.

My new editor at Dutton/Plume is Julia Serebrinsky, and the enthusiasm that she showed for this book from the very moment we discussed it over lunch gave me the motivation to begin working on it even before *Claire's Classic American Vegetarian Cooking* was published! She is a joy to work with.

Many thanks to everyone at Penguin. It takes a huge effort by many talented people to make a good book, and I am grateful to everyone in production, sales, marketing, publicity (thank you, Sarah Hemphill and Lisa Johnson), and the warehouse (special thanks to Gene Arlotta) and to the many book buyers who stock my books.

Carol Abel, my agent, has helped me a great deal along the way—thank you so much.

I don't even know how to begin to thank Frank, the great love of my life, for the tremendous help that he provided every day I worked on the recipes for this book. He was by my side, setting up the ingredients for each recipe, and keeping me focused. I could not have done it without him.

Special thanks to my Aunt Rose, Teresa Amendola McClure, Carole Amendola Meoli, and the many people both here in America and in Italy who so generously shared their recipes and their stories with me. They help to keep our Italian heritage alive through the celebrations at which foods play such an integral role in passing cherished traditions on to future generations. We'd surely be lost without this delicious link to the past. Thank you all from the bottom of my heart.

Above all, I give thanks and praise to God.

Contents

Introduction

This book contains 165 recipes, mainly from the wealth of family dishes that were always served at my grandmother's house, where I spent the first five years of my life and thousands of other days until she died when I was twenty-two years old. In our family, as in most Italian homes, love was served on the platters.

My mom, who is one of the greatest cooks I know, worked in a sewing machine factory when I was a child, and I spent my days with Grandma. For me, that meant mornings of homemade eggnog with just an added drop or two of espresso, enjoyed with slices of toasted Italian bread for dunking. Using a fork, Grandma would beat a fresh egg yolk in a coffee cup and add just the right amount of sugar. We sat together at the kitchen table, and I looked into the cup and watched the yolk change from bright yellow to a creamy pale yellow. Then Grandma would bring a little white enamel pot of heated milk from the stove and slowly pour it in while continuing to slowly swirl the mixture with the fork as it foamed slightly. Next she would add a drop of pure vanilla and a drop or two of espresso and tell me that I was getting so big that I could have a little *caffè*, just like Grandma. And that was only the beginning of the day's culinary adventure.

My grandmother was born in Amalfi, Italy, and came to America with her family when she was fourteen years old. They settled in New Haven, Connecticut, in a neighborhood where many more Amalfitanas would follow. My grandmother went to school in America and learned to speak English—with the most beautiful Italian accent. She met Paolo Bigio, who was also from Amalfi, when she was in her late teens, and on September 3, 1910, they were married. They opened a small market, and within a few years it had expanded along with their family. They moved to Wooster Street, where their brood grew to include seven children, and their market, located on the bottom floor of their three-family house, flourished over four decades. My family lived in one of the apartments in the house; my Uncle Jim and Aunt Rose lived in another; and Grandma was next door too. There is no doubt about it: the combination of living in the same building with my grandmother and aunt, who were marvelous cooks, so near a family-owned market, determined my destiny—my love and passion for good food!

A little bit of Amalfi came to America, right to the kitchen at Grandma's. The delicious foods of her birthplace stayed with her, and she passed the recipes on to her children.

Special celebrations and holidays were the highlights of my culinary experience. Our Christmas Eve dinners included antipasto platters of Fried Sweet and Hot Peppers (p. 27), Grilled Eggplant Slices (p. 64), White Bean and Mint Salad (p. 96), Caponata (p. 62), and Marinated Mushrooms and Olives (pp. 41–42). There were platters of Cipolline Fritte (Fried Little Onions) (p. 57), served with those little nuggets of peppery biscuits called Friselle (p. 37). And each year on February 3, we had our throats blessed at church to celebrate St. Blaise Day, then went home to eat Cornmeal Loaves with Raisins and Fennel Seeds (p. 165). Wait until you taste the Chocolate-Covered Eggplant (p. 215) that we made each August to celebrate the Feast of the Assumption!

Each region in Italy has foods that are specific to it. The favorites in our family include rich tomato sauces, bountiful antipasto platters with marinated vegetables, and dishes that use fresh lemon juice. Years later, when I visited Amalfi and saw ripe red tomatoes and lemon trees growing in great abundance, I knew exactly why our recipes were defined by them. They were a familiar part of the past, linking our family to its roots in Amalfi, passed to us via Grandma's kitchen.

Although my grandmother (and my mother as well) served many meatless meals, which are common in southern Italy, they also made some marvelous traditional favorites with meat. I must confess that I have enthusiastically consumed more than my share of their Italian meat loaf, their meatballs simmered in basil-scented tomato sauce, and their chicken cutlets Milanese or cacciatore style when I was growing up. A traditional meatball-filled lasagne is still a part of our Easter celebration.

You might wonder how I can keep a vegetarian diet and continue to enjoy meatball-filled lasagne at Easter, Italian meat loaf or hot dogs in split pea soup, or Italian hamburgers. Actually, it is quite easy, thanks to what I call the "new meats." Generally soy or wheat based, these delicious, healthful alternatives have a texture, taste, and appearance similar to familiar meats like beef, sausage, hot dogs, and chicken, and they are widely available. So on those occasions when meat is needed for a particular recipe, such as lentil and sausage stew, I use plant-based vegetarian meat. Wait until you taste my meat loaf! I know that my grandmother would be pleased.

Seitan, a wheat meat that has been used for centuries, is a new ingredient for many, so I will guide you through the steps necessary to make it. If you prefer to buy prepared seitan, you'll easily find it in health foods stores, but as with many other foods, the homemade version is so much better that I hope you'll at least try making it. Seitan looks, cooks, and even tastes like meat. Think of it as plant meat and a healthful natural food. (Remember how people thought frozen yogurt and kiwifruit were weird when they first became available?) If something tastes good, it will catch on, and I believe seitan will. To give it a try, dazzle your taste buds with Seitan Milanese (p. 206).

In keeping with our family tradition of cooking with the freshest, highest-quality ingredients while preserving the heritage of my Italian culture, I lovingly follow the recipes from my past and continue to use the finest ingredients available. There is no doubt in my mind that plant-based meats are better for you than any of the other meats on the market. You, too, are going to feel good about serving them.

When I look back on my childhood, my most precious memories involve the family, and these loving memories took place around the kitchen table. Even today, when I visit my mom's house, I know that my favorite dishes, prepared with love, will warm my heart and invigorate my palate. I always look forward to a plate of lightly fried zucchini cutlets, or in August a chocolate-covered eggplant to celebrate the Assumption. Family birthdays are celebrated with a special dessert, a sponge cake with strawberries and whipped cream filling. And my nieces and nephew know that they can look forward to roasted sweet potatoes (for Lisa and Carley) and roasted white potatoes (for Branden and Carolyn). Of course, there is always a pasta with marinara sauce because the kids look for that dish at Grandma's.

This book is as much about the loving memories of growing up in an Italian family as it is about the actual cooking that goes on in the heart of the Italian home—the kitchen. I want to share with you the many delicious ways we celebrate every special occasion, every holiday, every season with specific foods. I can't imagine an Easter without Minestra (p. 72), Barley Pie (p. 218), or Easter Sweet Bread (p. 217), or a Christmas without Anginettes (p. 234). A bridal shower wouldn't be the same without Pignoli Cookies (p. 220), and there must be pumpkin squash and red kidney beans during every fall season.

I hope this book will encourage you to make the kitchen the heart of your home and celebrate by cooking delicious vegetarian foods for your families and friends and neighbors—for everyone you love. I leave you with the same message my grandfather always left for me—*Statte buono*—which in the dialect of Amalfi means "Stay well."

Stocking the Italian Pantry

You'll find it much easier to cook from this book if you stock your pantry with basic Italian ingredients. Then you can jump right in and begin to savor the many traditional flavors that make Italian food the best-loved cuisine in America.

Shelf Items

Extra virgin olive oil (for sauces, soups, and dressings)
Olive oil (for medium-high-temperature cooking, light frying)
Canola oil
Balsamic vinegar
Red wine vinegar
White wine: Soave, Pinot Grigio, Chardonnay, Frascati
Red wine: Chianti, Valpolicella, Barola, Bardolino, Cabernet
Sweet and dry vermouth
Olives: oil-cured black, Kalamata, Spanish, green
Capers
Peperoncini peppers (sold in jars)
Hot cherry peppers (sold in jars)
Artichoke hearts (canned)
Tomato paste (6-ounce cans)

Italian whole peeled tomatoes in juice (28-ounce and 35-ounce cans)
Italian crushed tomatoes
Italian tomato puree
Dried herbs and spices: basil, oregano, rosemary, fennel seeds, mint, sage, thyme, bay
    leaves, red pepper flakes, ground red pepper, black peppercorns
Assorted dried beans: chickpeas, great northern, red kidney, cannellini, lentils,
    split peas, fava
Assorted pastas: pastina (little pasta dots), penne, ziti, linguine, angel hair,
    tubetti, gnocchi, orecchiette, tagliatelle, and other favorites
Arborio rice
Cornmeal
Plain bread crumbs
Almonds (slivered, sliced, and whole)
Pine nuts
Pure vanilla, lemon, and almond extracts
Dried fruits: raisins, dates, cherries, chestnuts, figs

Frozen Foods

The following new vegetarian ingredients are used to give my recipes the traditional
meaty flavors and textures that until recently were available only from animal meat
protein. They are all readily available from health foods stores and in many supermarkets, usually in the frozen foods section or in the refrigerated produce depart-
ment. I buy several packages of each so that I can have them on hand.

Ground Meatless by Worthington Morningstar Foods
Gimme Lean "Beef" by Lightlife
Ground "Beef" Crumbles by Green Giant
Vegetarian Burgers, Harvest Burgers (Original) by Green Giant
Lean Italian Links meatless sausages by Lightlife
Seitan, traditionally seasoned wheat gluten, by White Wave
Fakin' Bacon by Lightlife
Vegetarian Pepperoni by Yves
Vegetarian Hot Dogs (New Menu) by VitaSoy, or Vegetarian Hot Dogs by
    Worthington, White Wave, Lightlife, or Yves

Italian Cheeses

If you have not yet tried imported Italian cheeses, then you are in for a delicious experience. Several of the recipes in this cookbook call for the following cheeses. Please note that most cheeses produced in Italy contain animal rennet. Many American made cheeses do not. Soyco brand makes a dairy-free Parmesan alternative called Soymage. To verify the ingredients you'll need to contact the individual manufacturers.

Gorgonzola is a rich and creamy cow's milk cheese. It has blue-green streaks running through it and a pungent flavor that goes well with pears. It is also a perfect accompaniment to a glass of port or a Chianti Reserve.

Ricotta salata is a sheep's milk cheese that is firm enough to grate or cut into cubes or slices. It is a good alternative to grated pecorino Romano cheese for topping pasta and sauce. Ricotta salata pairs nicely with tomatoes.

Asiago is a semifirm cheese made from cow's milk. Its nutty taste adds a rich flavor to pizza toppings and salads.

Pecorino Romano is a sheep's milk cheese with a sharp flavor. Buy it in pieces and grate it fresh over pasta and sauce, or use a potato peeler to slice curls to top tossed salads.

Parmigiano-Reggiano is made with cow's milk, usually partially skimmed. This pale yellow cheese is best when freshly grated. It makes a fine addition to lasagne fillings of ricotta and mozzarella, and it is delicious sprinkled over pizzas and pastas. The nutty, buttery flavor is slightly saltier and less sharp than pecorino Romano. Try combining freshly grated Parmigiano-Reggiano with freshly grated pecorino Romano. The flavor is delicious and will give you the best of both cheeses.

Mozzarella is available in many forms. The rubbery commercial product available in supermarkets is the most familiar and really does fine when you are in a pinch. The fresher, *fiore di latte* ("flower of milk") mozzarella is packed in the milk (the whey) from the mozzarella and is a softer, more beautifully textured, more flavorful mozzarella. It melts more evenly, and once you taste the difference, you'll never want the rubbery blocks again. Slices of fresh mozzarella make a fine salad—just alternate the mozzarella with slices of fresh tomato and basil leaves, drizzle with extra virgin olive oil, and sprinkle with a little salt and pepper. You will have a delicious simple salad that I highly recommend for a light lunch along with good Italian bread and maybe a glass of chilled lemonade if it's a warm day.

Most supermarkets now carry *bocconcini*, which are little balls of fresh mozzarella that are perfect in salads or pastas, and they can be marinated in extra virgin olive oil with fresh herbs (rosemary, basil, and oregano) and a little salt and pepper for an easy and delicious appetizer. Just serve with toothpicks for plucking one out of the marinade. Buffalo mozzarella (*mozzarella di bufala*) is made with the milk of the water buffalo, the way all mozzarella was originally made in Italy. The flavor is astoundingly delicious, but this specialty mozzarella commands a high price. It is well worth it for special occasions. High-quality (pricey) Italian markets will carry it. Also try smoked mozzarella (*mozzarella affumicata*). Its smoky flavor is wonderful in risotto, melted on sandwiches, and on pizzas.

Ricotta means "recooked," and this cheese is made from the whey that comes off in the process of making mozzarella cheese. Maybe that's why ricotta and mozzarella are so delicious together. Use ricotta cheese in lasagne and manicotti or in baked macaroni and cheese, or add dollops on top of your favorite pasta with sauce. In our family we sometimes mix a few spoonfuls of ricotta into a bowl of pasta with marinara sauce; it adds a light sweetness and creamy flavor. Add a little sugar to this delicately flavored cheese and you have a lovely spread for toast.

Italian Wines

I like to pair an Italian meal with an Italian wine, and with the many choices of good Italian wines that are available today, we don't have to settle for the familiar Chianti in a basket. The following are some of my favorites. I highly recommend that you keep a journal and make notes about the wines that you buy, rating how you enjoy them and what you ate along with each one. This will help you plan future meals. We do this at home and find it helpful, especially because it's easy to forget the winery name with so many out there. Robust red wine like a Chianti Riserva (Reserve) is my favorite, especially with cheeses or a pasta dish in a sauce of San Marzano tomatoes. I do enjoy a lighter white wine during the hot summer months when I tend to eat lighter foods.

RED WINES

Chianti is produced in the Tuscan region of Italy. "Riserva" indicates a higher-quality Chianti that has been aged in oak for at least three years. This method yields a robust flavor that pairs well with assertive flavors such as hearty red sauces and rich cheeses.

Barola is a robust red wine produced in the Piedmont region of Italy. It resembles a Cabernet and its full body pairs nicely with foods of bold flavors just like a Chianti.

Valpolicella and **Bardolino** are light, fruity red wines that are produced in the northern Italian regions. These wines are meant to be consumed within a few years of production because as time goes by the flavor becomes more dry. I like to pair these wines with lighter soups, salads, and appetizers.

WHITE WINES

Pinot Grigio is a crisp, dry white wine, not quite as buttery as a Chardonnay because very little wood is used in fermentation. Pinot Grigio wines are gentle and enhance the flavor of just about any kind of meal.

Frascati is a light inexpensive table wine with an earthy, fruity flavor. It is slightly effervescent and great with pasta.

Gavi di Gavi is a white wine from Gavi, Italy. This exquisite wine is made from the Cortese grape, which is light and somewhat acidic. It's great with any dish made with olive oil or butter, but not with vinegar.

Tips on Beans

There is a growing interest in beans, and I couldn't be happier about it. Beans are packed with protein, and are also a rich source of both soluble and insoluble fiber, something our bodies desperately need. Adding fiber to our diet is important, because research studies conclude that if we consume 30 grams of fiber a day, we can decrease our cholesterol level, reduce heart disease, and prevent colon cancer. By adding just 1/2 cup of cooked beans to your diet, you can boost your fiber by an average of 10 grams, and that is one-third of the fiber you need in a whole day. Add cooked beans to tossed salad at lunch or dinner for extra flavor and crunch. Eat a bean soup, salad, or sauce every day. All my cookbooks provide plenty of recipes that use beans. They are a big part of my diet, my restaurant menu, and certainly of the Italian kitchen.

If you haven't utilized beans extensively, add them to your diet gradually. Start out with only a couple of tablespoons a day. Remember that when you add any extra fiber to your diet, you need to drink enough water to wash the fiber down.

As you will see in my recipes, I don't presoak dried beans. Actually, I had never heard of soaking beans until I wrote my first cookbook. People began phoning me at the restaurant, asking, "When do you soak the beans?" My grandmother and my mom didn't presoak, and I don't either. Although I don't have any scientific documentation to support my theory, I do have an average of four hundred customers each day (for longer than twenty-three years), and we cook an average of 30 pounds of beans each day in our soups, salads, and entrees. I believe that cooking beans longer may reduce the difficulty in digestion that many people experience.

Dried beans should always be picked over for any stones before they are cooked. I find it easiest to spread a single layer of beans on a white dinner plate. Any stones will stand out more easily. Cooking times will occasionally vary depending on the variety and on the age of the bean. The longer it is dried, the harder it is. To cook dried beans separately for a salad or dip, place 1 pound of picked-over beans in a large heavy pot. When cooking beans always use a heavy pot to prevent sticking. A thin stock pot won't do. Add 3 quarts of cold water, cover the pot, and bring to a boil over high heat. Reduce the heat and cook at a low boil for 1 hour. Then begin testing for doneness every 15 minutes or so until they are tender. You don't even need to stir them; in fact, it's better not to disturb them, as you'll break the skins. If your lid doesn't fit tightly and the water evaporates too quickly, just add more water to keep the beans covered by at least 2 inches of water at all times. Add salt during the last half hour of cooking because it has a tendency to toughen the skins. After your beans are cooked to your preference, drain them in a colander, then let them cool to room temperature. Store them in the refrigerator in a covered container for up to 4 days or freeze them for up to 1 month.

A Few Words on Pastas

Pastas are vital to the southern Italian pantry, so I want to share some tips with you about how to select and cook them. I prefer to buy imported pastas because they are made with durum wheat, a hard wheat that is ground into semolina flour. Semolina produces a sturdy pasta that maintains its shape during cooking. Many American pastas are made with a combination of hard and soft wheats, and the final product is less sturdy and often doesn't hold its shape. You'll appreciate this, especially when cooking farfalle (bow ties), which turn to rectangles if you use some American brands.

If you are buying American-made pastas, look for those made with 100 percent semolina.

Every family has its favorite pastas and shapes. When I make a sauce that has green peas or other little pieces of vegetables, I often choose a medium pasta shell to collect little "spoonfuls" of flavor. But if I am in the mood for spaghetti, I can toss it with the sauce. It's all a matter of preference.

When cooking pastas, start out with plenty of cold water (4 quarts per pound of pasta). Bring the water to a rapid boil in a large pot over high heat. Covering the pot is efficient—it allows the water to boil more quickly and keeps your kitchen cooler. When the water reaches a rapid boil, stir in a teaspoon or two of salt. Add the pasta, stirring with a wooden spoon as you add it. A wooden spoon is gentler on pasta then a metal spoon.

Continue stirring the pasta until the water returns to a boil. This will prevent the pasta from sticking, which is especially important when cooking spaghetti, angel hair pasta, or any other strands. Follow the package instructions for cooking time, stirring occasionally during cooking.

Test the pasta for doneness. It should be sufficiently firm before it is drained in a colander. Make sure you drain it thoroughly.

After I cook the pasta, I return it, well drained, to the pot. I ladle a little sauce over it and toss with two wooden spoons to coat the strands. Tossing the pasta with sauce allows the flavors to absorb evenly into the pasta. Turn the pasta into a serving bowl and then ladle additional sauce over it.

If you must prepare pasta in advance, run it under cold water after you drain it to remove the excess starch. Otherwise, the strands (or pieces) will stick together. Drain the pasta again. To prevent it from sticking further, turn the pasta into a container and toss it with a teaspoon of olive oil. You can refrigerate it for up to 2 days without affecting the flavor. This procedure also works well when you are making a pasta salad. It is better, however, to cook the pasta fresh when you are serving it with a sauce, because the starches allow the sauce to stick to the strands and absorb the flavors of the sauce.

Special Menus for Popular Holidays and Celebrations

There are many reasons to celebrate, and in our family, as in so many Italian American families, food is at the center of a gathering. We've come to expect certain foods on specific occasions, and the tradition is a joy to pass on. These are some of my favorites, and I hope you will include them in your celebrations.

Religious Holidays

CHRISTMAS EVE (THE FRYING HOLIDAY)

Crispy Oyster Mushrooms (page 24)
Fried Onion Slices (page 40)
Fried Carrots and Parsnips (page 28)

CHRISTMAS DINNER

Holiday Lasagne (page 144)
Caponata (page 62)
Anginettes (page 234)
Fried Struffoli (page 221)
Pignoli Cookies (page 220)

Easter Sunday

Minestra (page 72)
Holiday Lasagne (page 144) or Homemade Manicotti (page 132)
Pan-Seared Herb-Crusted Portobello Mushrooms (page 188)
Baby Artichokes with Lemon-Caper Stuffing (page 17)
Barley Pie (page 218)
Easter Sweet Bread (page 217)

St. Blaise Day (February 3)

Cornmeal Loaves with Raisins and Fennel Seeds (page 165)

Feast of the Assumption (August 15)

Chocolate-Covered Eggplant (page 215)

Secular Celebrations

Child's Birthday Party

Pizza Amalfitan Style (page 166)
Ice Box Cake (page 230)

Summer Luncheon

Bacon, Arugula, and Tomato on Italian Bread with Basil Mayonnaise (page 103)
Italian Potato Salad (page 91)
Italian Fruit Salad (page 228)

Sunday Dinner

Potato Gnocchi (page 118)
Seitan Milanese (page 206)
Amalfitan-Style Mashed Potatoes (page 32)
Artichoke Hearts Francese (page 16)
Broccoli Salad (page 100)
Cream Puffs (page 233)

OUTDOOR CONCERT AT THE TOWN GREEN

Antipasto Platter: Baby Artichokes with Lemon-Caper Stuffing (page 17),
Marinated Mushrooms (page 41), Marinated Olives (page 42), Goat Cheese with
Olive Oil and Herbs (page 19)
Sun-Dried Tomato Muffins (page 55)
Friselle (Little Pepper Nuggets) (page 37)
Anisette Dunking Cookies (page 237) with Anisette Glaze (page 238)
Thermos of espresso

Antipasti, Appetizers, and Side Dishes

The fine line that once existed between an appetizer and a side dish has all but been erased in my house. I find that my family and guests are quite satisfied when I serve foods that used to be traditional side dishes, such as Fried Sweet and Hot Peppers (page 27), Roasted Potatoes with Rosemary and Garlic (page 34), or even Amalfitan-Style Mashed Potatoes (page 32) or Sautéed Broccoli Rabe (page 39) as appetizers. Appetizers have become little plates of just about anything, and they can be served before the meal or as the meal.

Side dishes play a dual role in today's diet. When they are served before a meal, they are thought of more as appetizers. On some occasions several side dishes may be served as the meal. In fact, we occasionally choose several side dishes when we entertain groups of friends for a casual dinner party.

An antipasto (Italian for "before the pasta") platter is traditionally served as the first course on special occasions and on holidays when we have extra time to cook and to eat and when we are having a more formal dinner. I occasionally even bring along a large platter of antipasto to our local cabaret theatre.

Antipasti, Appetizers, and Side Dishes

Artichoke Hearts Francese
Baby Artichokes with Lemon-Caper Stuffing

Goat Cheese with Olive Oil and Herbs
White Bean Spread
Sautéed Escarole with Garlic Chips and Red Pepper Flakes
Sauté of Zucchini, Plum Tomatoes, and Sweet Onion
Pizza with Goat Cheese and Truffle Oil
Crispy Oyster Mushrooms
Roasted Potatoes, Beets, and Cipolline with Olive Oil and Balsamic Vinegar
Fried Sweet and Hot Peppers
Fried Carrots and Parsnips
Chicory and Potatoes
Roasted-Garlic Mashed Potatoes
Potato Cakes
Amalfitan-Style Mashed Potatoes
Roasted Potatoes with Rosemary and Garlic
Spiedini
Friselle (Little Pepper Nuggets)
Stewed Red, Green, and Cubanelle Peppers
Sautéed Broccoli Rabe
Fried Onion Slices
Marinated Mushrooms
Marinated Olives
Artichokes Baked with Asiago Cheese
Beets and Potatoes with Carrots
Sautéed Carrots with Onions and Green Peas
Sautéed Mushrooms
Mushrooms with Lemon, White Wine, and Parsley
Roasted Portobello Mushrooms with Mint and Garlic
Porcini Mushroom Gravy
Stewed Leeks and Tomatoes with White Wine
Sautéed Fennel
Sautéed Endive
Sautéed Radicchio
Sautéed Spinach
Sun-Dried Tomato Muffins
Onion-Parmesan Puffs
Cipolline Fritte (Fried Little Onions)
Peas and Cipolline with Meatless Bacon

Chickpeas with Tomatoes and Rosemary
Green Beans Stewed with Tomatoes
Caponata
Sautéed Eggplant
Grilled Eggplant Slices

Artichoke Hearts Francese

SERVES 6

For me, anything prepared Francese style—that is, made with butter, white wine, lemon juice, and sometimes capers—is a rich and wonderful treat. If you love artichoke hearts, you might want to double the recipe. Be sure to spoon the luscious juices over the artichoke hearts as you serve them.

> 1 (14-ounce) can artichoke hearts, drained
> 1/2 cup unbleached all-purpose flour
>   Salt and pepper to taste
> 3 eggs
> 1/4 cup olive oil
> 1/4 cup dry white wine
> 3 tablespoons fresh lemon juice (about 1 lemon)
> 1 tablespoon capers, drained
> 3 tablespoons butter, cut into small pieces
> 1 tablespoon finely chopped flat-leaf parsley

1. Cut the artichoke hearts into halves or into quarters if they are large. Measure the flour into a shallow bowl and season with salt and pepper. In a deep bowl, beat the eggs lightly with a fork and season with salt and pepper.

2. Set a platter by the bowl of flour. Dredge the artichoke hearts in the seasoned flour, shake off the excess, then arrange them on the platter.

3. Heat the oil in a large skillet over medium heat. Working quickly, dip one artichoke heart at a time into the beaten eggs, then place it in the heated oil. Continue with the remaining artichoke hearts. Cook for 2 to 3 minutes, or until golden brown. Using tongs, turn each artichoke heart and cook the other side for 2 to 3 minutes, or until golden brown.

4. Pour the wine and lemon juice evenly over the artichoke hearts, then scatter the capers on top. Sprinkle with salt and pepper. Cover and cook for 1 minute, carefully rotating the skillet to move the liquid.

5. Add the pieces of butter, carefully moving the skillet to mix in the butter as it melts. Cover and cook for 1 to 2 minutes, or until the sauce thickens slightly. Taste for seasonings. Place the artichokes in a serving bowl and pour the sauce over, using a rubber spatula to scrape the juices from the skillet. Scatter the parsley on top.

Baby Artichokes with Lemon~Caper Stuffing

Serves 6

Baby artichokes are available during several seasons, mainly in late winter/early spring, again in late summer, and also late in the fall. In this recipe you can serve them either warm or chilled because the lemon- and caper-flavored bread stuffing tastes delicious either way.

1 lemon
3 large cloves garlic, minced
6 baby artichokes (about 1¹/₄ pounds)
  Salt and pepper to taste
6 (1-inch-thick) slices Italian bread
2 tablespoons tiny (nonpareil) capers, drained
1 tablespoon olive oil
1 tablespoon minced flat-leaf parsley
1 egg

1. Bring a large pot of lightly salted water to a boil over high heat.

2. Grate 1 tablespoon of zest from the lemon and reserve. Cut the lemon in half. Squeeze the juice from half of the lemon into the pot of water. Squeeze the juice from the other half and reserve. Add one-third of the minced garlic to the pot.

3. Trim the stems from the artichokes, chop the stems finely, and reserve.

4. When the water comes to a boil, add the artichokes, salt, and pepper. Cover and cook for 15 to 18 minutes, or until the artichokes are barely tender. Test for doneness by pulling a leaf from an artichoke; if it comes off easily, it's ready. Drain the artichokes.

5. While the artichokes are cooking, place the bread in a bowl. Cover it with hot tap water. When the bread is cool enough to handle, place it in a colander. Squeeze out as much water as possible, using your hand to push the bread against the colander.

6. Place the drained bread in a bowl. Add the reserved lemon zest, reserved lemon juice, reserved artichoke stems, remaining minced garlic, capers, oil, parsley, egg, salt, and pepper. Stir to mix thoroughly. Taste for seasonings.

7. Preheat the oven to 350 degrees. When the artichokes are cool enough to handle, pull out the center leaves of each one to create a cavity for stuffing. Divide the stuffing evenly among the artichokes, packing it into the cavities.

8. Arrange the stuffed artichokes upright in a glass baking dish. Pour 1 cup of tap water around, not over, the artichokes. Cover the dish tightly with foil. Bake for 45 to 50 minutes, or until the stuffing is heated through and the leaves are tender to the bite. Serve hot or chilled.

Goat Cheese with Olive Oil and Herbs

SERVES 6

Little rounds of goat cheese drizzled with olive oil and sprinkled with fresh herbs are perfect served with garlic toasts or slices of crusty Italian bread. I recommend that you keep these treats on hand. They are perfect for a snack and go nicely with a glass of Chianti. You can store them in a covered butter dish in the refrigerator for up to a week.

1   (6- to 8-ounce) log firm goat cheese (chèvre), cut into $1/2$-inch-thick slices
3   tablespoons extra virgin olive oil
1   tablespoon fresh rosemary leaves
1   tablespoon chopped fresh oregano
    Salt and coarsely ground black pepper to taste

Arrange the goat cheese slices on a platter or in a butter dish, overlapping them slightly. Drizzle the oil evenly over the cheese. Scatter the rosemary and oregano evenly on top of the cheese and season with salt and pepper. Serve immediately or cover and refrigerate for up to a week.

White Bean Spread

MAKES ABOUT 1¹/₂ CUPS

I always keep a can of organic navy pea beans on hand to make this delicious spread for unexpected guests. Serve it with slices of toasted Italian bread for a healthy and quick appetizer. Any leftovers make a great sandwich filling for the next day's lunch when paired with sliced tomatoes and onion.

Note: I use smoked tempeh strips, Fakin' Bacon, by Lightlife Foods in this recipe. It is available in health foods stores and many supermarkets.

1   (15-ounce) can navy pea beans, drained (about 1³/₄ cups)
2   strips meatless bacon, chopped
3   large cloves garlic, coarsely chopped
3   tablespoons coarsely chopped flat-leaf parsley
1   tablespoon extra virgin olive oil
2   tablespoons fresh lemon juice (about 1 lemon)
    Salt and pepper to taste

1. Measure the ingredients into a food processor bowl. Cover and process for about 45 seconds, or until smooth.
2. Taste for seasoning.
3. Cover and refrigerate any unused spread for up to four days.

Sautéed Escarole with Garlic Chips and Red Pepper Flakes

SERVES 6

I can't imagine a week without this delicious, mildly bitter, versatile Italian green vegetable. Enjoy it as a side dish or cooked in a soup, in a vegetable pie, in calzones, or on a pizza.

1 large head escarole (about 1 pound)
2 tablespoons extra virgin olive oil
4 large cloves garlic, cut into thick slices
1/4 teaspoon red pepper flakes
2 tablespoons capers, drained
Salt and pepper to taste

1. Cut off and discard the bottom 1 inch of the escarole. Place the escarole leaves in a large bowl or sink of cool water and swish them around to loosen any sand. Lift the escarole into a colander, change the water in the bowl or sink, and repeat the process until all the sand is removed from the escarole. Drain the escarole in the colander.

2. Bring 2 quarts of lightly salted water to a boil in a large pot over high heat. Add the escarole, using tongs to push the leaves into the water. Cover and cook for 5 minutes, stirring occasionally. Drain the escarole in a colander.

3. Heat the oil in the pot over medium-low heat. Add the garlic, red pepper flakes, and capers. Cook, stirring frequently, for 3 minutes, or until the garlic is softened but not brown. Add the drained escarole. Sprinkle with salt and pepper. Turn to mix, using the tongs. Cover and continue cooking, stirring occasionally, for 5 to 8 minutes, or until the escarole is tender to your preference. Taste for seasonings.

Sauté of Zucchini, Plum Tomatoes, and Sweet Onion

SERVES 4

This delicious and colorful vegetable dish can be found in every southern Italian home. We serve it year-round but especially during the summer months when our garden is overflowing with zucchini and red, ripe tomatoes.

2 tablespoons extra virgin olive oil
2 large cloves garlic, coarsely chopped
1 large sweet onion, cut into thick rings
3 medium zucchini (about 12 ounces), cut into 1-inch chunks
4 ripe medium plum tomatoes, cut into quarters lengthwise
1/2 teaspoon dried oregano
Salt and pepper to taste
1/8 teaspoon ground red pepper

1. Heat the oil in a large skillet over medium heat. Add the garlic, onion, zucchini, and tomatoes. Sprinkle with the oregano, salt, black pepper, and red pepper. Stir to mix.

2. Cover and cook, stirring occasionally, for about 15 minutes, or until the zucchini is just tender. Taste for seasonings.

Pizza with Goat Cheese and Truffle Oil

MAKES 30 APPETIZER PIECES

Every Sunday during the cool months of the year, there was a big pot of pizza dough rising by the stove in our kitchen. My mom made pizzas, calzones, and vegetable rolls from her delicious dough. She still makes wonderful pizzas for us on many Sundays, but now she buys the pizza dough from our local pizza parlor. Although I miss the lovely sight of rising dough, I have to confess that the dough from the store can be delicious and is a real time-saver. Besides, it is the filling or topping that really makes the pizza.

This combination is a big hit. The nutty flavor of goat cheese pairs beautifully with the earthy flavor of truffle oil. Although truffle oil is pricey, it is still an economical way to savor the marvelous, earthy flavor of truffles, those rare jewels dug from the earth around particular trees in Italy or France. Buy a small bottle of truffle oil from a gourmet shop; it will last awhile.

2 **tablespoons unbleached all-purpose flour**
1 **pound pizza dough, thawed if frozen**
2 **tablespoons cornmeal**
8 **ounces goat cheese (chèvre), crumbled**
 Salt and pepper to taste
2 **tablespoons truffle oil**

1. Preheat the oven to 400 degrees. Spread the flour in a 12-inch circle on your countertop. Place the dough on the flour. Pat it gently with your fingertips, pushing slightly outward as you pat. Turn the dough over and coat the other side with flour.

2. Lightly dust a rolling pin with a little of the flour from the counter. Roll the dough into a 15 × 12-inch rectangle.

3. Spray a large cookie sheet with olive oil cooking spray. Scatter the cornmeal evenly over the sheet. Carefully transfer the dough to the cookie sheet. Reshape it if necessary with your fingertips.

4. Scatter the crumbled goat cheese evenly over the dough. Sprinkle lightly with salt and pepper. Drizzle the truffle oil evenly over the cheese.

5. Bake the pizza for 25 minutes, or until the crust is golden brown. Remove from the oven and cut into 30 pieces. Serve hot or at room temperature.

Crispy Oyster Mushrooms

MAKES APPROXIMATELY 25 PIECES

The kitchen is where I feel closest to my grandmother. and try to duplicate the many dishes she lovingly prepared for me. The crisp, spicy coating on these oyster mushrooms is much like that on the fried calamari my grandmother made each Christmas Eve when, like most Italians, we celebrated with a lavish fish and seafood dinner. The flavor is delicious and the memories are magical.

Note: Choose large oyster mushrooms 3 to 4 inches long, including stems. Serve these crispy treats with lemon wedges or marinara sauce for dipping.

8 ounces large oyster mushrooms
1/2 cup soy milk
1/8 teaspoon ground red pepper
Salt and pepper to taste
1 cup unbleached all-purpose flour
3 tablespoons Old Bay seasoning
1 tablespoon dried thyme
1/4 cup peanut oil
2 lemons, cut into wedges (optional)

1. Carefully separate each mushroom from the bunch, keeping the mushroom and stem intact. Rinse the mushrooms gently to remove any surface dirt. Drain on a double layer of paper towels.

2. Measure the soy milk into a shallow bowl. Sprinkle with half of the red pepper and a little salt and black pepper. Whisk to combine. In a separate shallow bowl, combine the flour, Old Bay seasoning, remaining red pepper, thyme, and a little salt and pepper. Whisk to mix.

3. Set a cookie sheet near the soy milk and flour mixtures. Holding an oyster mushroom by its stem, dip it into the soy milk mixture to coat. Shake off the excess. Carefully dredge the mushroom in the flour mixture, turning to coat evenly. Shake off the excess. Place the coated mushroom on the cookie sheet. Repeat the process with all of the mushrooms.

4. Heat the oil in a large nonstick skillet over medium-high heat. Place a

tray lined with a double layer of paper towels by the stove. Arrange as many mushrooms as you can in a single layer in the hot oil without crowding. Cook the mushrooms for 3 to 4 minutes on each side, or until golden brown. Transfer the browned mushrooms to the towel-lined tray. Continue cooking the remaining mushrooms. Serve with lemon wedges if desired.

Roasted Potatoes, Beets, and Cipolline with Olive Oil and Balsamic Vinegar

SERVES 6

Cipolline are wild little Italian onions. They have a sweet yet sharp onion flavor and are showing up in supermarkets across the country. They combine beautifully when roasted with potatoes and fresh beets, and balsamic vinegar is a perfect foil for the combination of sweet and pungent flavors.

4 large baking potatoes, unpeeled
3 large fresh beets
6 cipolline, peeled
6 large cloves garlic, peeled
2 tablespoons extra virgin olive oil
2 tablespoons balsamic vinegar
2 tablespoons fresh rosemary leaves
Salt and pepper to taste

1. Preheat the oven to 375 degrees. Cut the potatoes lengthwise into 6 wedges. Peel and quarter the beets. Place the potatoes, beets, cipolline, and garlic in a large bowl. Drizzle the olive oil evenly over the vegetables. Toss well to coat.

2. Drizzle the balsamic vinegar and scatter the rosemary leaves evenly over the vegetables. Sprinkle with salt and pepper and toss well to coat.

3. Spray a rectangular baking pan with olive oil cooking spray. Turn the vegetables into the pan, using a rubber spatula to scrape out the bowl. Spread the vegetables evenly and cover the pan tightly with foil. Bake the vegetables for 1 hour, or until the beets are just tender when tested with a fork.

Fried Sweet and Hot Peppers

SERVES 6

This is a great side dish for those who enjoy the intense flavor of fiery-hot peppers tempered and complemented by plump sweet red peppers. In our house we eat plenty of these peppers with Italian bread.

2 **tablespoons extra virgin olive oil**
6 **large cloves garlic, sliced in half**
2 **large sweet onions, cut into 1/2-inch-wide ribs**
6 **long (about 7 inches) hot green peppers (about 8 ounces)**
4 **large red bell peppers, seeded and sliced into 1/2-inch-wide ribs**
   Salt and pepper to taste
1 **tablespoon chopped fresh oregano or 11/2 teaspoons dried**

Heat the oil in a large skillet over medium heat. Add the garlic, onions, hot peppers, and bell peppers. Sprinkle with salt and pepper and oregano. Cover and cook for about 20 minutes, or until the peppers are tender and the onions are golden brown. It is helpful to use tongs for turning the peppers until they are soft enough to stir with a spoon. Lower the heat to medium-low if the vegetables begin to stick. Taste for seasonings.

Fried Carrots and Parsnips

SERVES 6

These crispy vegetables are terrific as a side dish or as part of a fried mixed vegetable platter called fritto misto. *Serve them with lemon wedges.*

4 medium parsnips, peeled and cut into 1/3-inch-thick diagonal slices
5 medium carrots, peeled and cut into 1/4-inch-thick diagonal slices
   Salt and pepper to taste
1 cup unbleached all-purpose flour
4 eggs, lightly beaten
1/4 cup finely chopped flat-leaf parsley
2 cups plain dry bread crumbs
1/2 cup olive oil
1 lemon, cut into 6 wedges

1. Bring 3 quarts of water to a boil in a large pot over high heat. Add the parsnips, carrots, salt, and pepper. Cover and cook for 5 minutes, or until crisp-tender. Drain and set aside until cool enough to handle.

2. While the parsnips and carrots are cooling, measure the flour into a bowl. Beat the eggs in a separate bowl. Add the parsley, salt, and pepper to the eggs. Measure the bread crumbs into a third bowl.

3. Dredge a slice of parsnip in the flour, coating it thoroughly, then shake off the excess. Dip it into the beaten eggs and shake off the excess. Coat the parsnip slice with bread crumbs and place it on a cookie sheet. Repeat with all of the parsnip and carrot slices.

4. Line a large platter or a cookie sheet with a double layer of paper towels. Set it by the stove.

5. Heat 1/4 cup of the oil in a large nonstick skillet over medium-high heat. Arrange as many parsnip or carrot slices as you can in a single layer in the skillet without crowding. Cook each side for about 2 minutes, or until medium brown, using tongs to turn. Transfer to the towel-lined platter.

6. Continue cooking batches of the remaining parsnip and carrot slices, adding the remaining 1/4 cup oil as needed. To serve, arrange the cooked carrots and parsnips on a platter. Serve with the lemon wedges.

Chicory and Potatoes

SERVES 6

My love of greens comes from my grandmother, who, like most Italians, favored chicory, escarole, arugula, dandelion, and rabe. We use chicory, a slightly bitter member of the endive family, in salads as well as in many vegetable soups and in this lovely sautéed dish. Serve it with plenty of Italian bread for sopping up the delicious juices.

3   tablespoons extra virgin olive oil
3   large cloves garlic, cut into thick slices
4   large baking potatoes, peeled and sliced into 1/4-inch-thick rounds
1   rib celery, cut into thin slices
2   large heads chicory (about 2 pounds), bottom 2 inches trimmed off, cut into 2-inch pieces
    Salt and pepper to taste
1/4 cup coarsely chopped fresh mint
1/2 cup water
3   tablespoons fresh lemon juice (about 1 lemon)

1. Heat the oil in a large pot over medium-low heat. Add the garlic, potatoes, celery, chicory, salt, pepper, and mint. Toss to coat the ingredients with the oil. Cover and cook, stirring frequently, for 5 to 8 minutes, or until the chicory is wilted.

2. Add the water, stirring well to mix. Cover and continue cooking, stirring occasionally, for about 20 minutes (the mixture will come to a boil after about 5 minutes), or until the potatoes are tender when tested with a fork. Stir in the lemon juice. Taste for seasonings.

Roasted-Garlic Mashed Potatoes

SERVES 6 OR MORE

It's a good idea to keep a supply of roasted garlic in your refrigerator. You can use it to add a delicious, somewhat mellow garlic flavor to many foods. I like stirring a couple of cloves into salad dressings, mayonnaise, pasta sauces, and creamy mashed potatoes. Covered in a bowl, the roasted garlic will keep well for 4 to 5 days. Leftover mashed potatoes are great for making Potato Cakes (page 31).

> 3 large cloves garlic, unpeeled
> 2 tablespoons extra virgin olive oil
>   Salt and pepper to taste
> 1 small yellow onion, finely chopped
> 6 medium baking potatoes, peeled and cut into eighths
> 1 cup milk or soy milk

1. Preheat the oven to 350 degrees. Place the unpeeled garlic cloves in a bowl. Drizzle 1/2 teaspoon of the oil evenly over the garlic. Sprinkle with salt and pepper. Toss to coat the cloves.

2. Arrange the garlic cloves on a 12-inch length of foil, leaving an inch or so of space between them. Bake for 20 to 23 minutes, or until the garlic is soft to the touch. Set aside until cool enough to squeeze the softened clove of garlic from its peel; it should come out easily.

3. While the garlic is roasting, heat the remaining oil in a small skillet over medium heat. Add the onion, salt, and pepper. Cook for 5 minutes, stirring occasionally, until the onion is golden brown but not burned. Set aside.

4. Bring a large pot of lightly salted water to a boil over high heat. Add the potatoes, cover, and cook for about 12 minutes, or until soft when tested with a fork. Reserve 1/2 cup of the water before draining the potatoes.

5. Return the drained potatoes to the pot. Add the roasted garlic, sautéed onions (use a rubber spatula to scrape the skillet of juices and olive oil), the reserved 1/2 cup of water from cooking the potatoes, and the milk. Mash the potatoes until smooth and creamy. Taste for seasonings.

Potato Cakes

MAKES 9 POTATO CAKES

When I was growing up, my mom made huge batches of creamy mashed potatoes at least once a week. Leftovers were destined to become log-shaped potato croquettes (the recipe is in Claire's Corner Copia Cookbook) *or these potato cakes. Sometimes I don't even wait for leftovers but prepare mashed potatoes exclusively for these potato cakes. Although any recipe for mashed potatoes will work nicely, I like to use Roasted-Garlic Mashed Potatoes. Serve the potato cakes with Italian Hamburgers (page 191) or any veggie burgers and a tossed salad for a delicious supper.*

> 3 **cups Roasted-Garlic Mashed Potatoes (page 30)**
> 3 **eggs**
> 1/4 **cup finely chopped flat-leaf parsley**
>   **Salt and pepper to taste**
> 1 1/2 **cups plain dry bread crumbs**
> 1/4 **cup olive oil**

1. Using your hands, form the chilled or room-temperature mashed potatoes into 9 little cakes (a 1/3-cup measure is handy for measuring out the potatoes). Arrange on a cookie sheet.

2. Break the eggs into a shallow bowl. Add the parsley, salt, and pepper. Beat together with a fork or a whisk.

3. Measure the bread crumbs into a shallow bowl. Carefully (the potatoes are soft) dip a potato cake into the beaten eggs to coat both sides. Gently shake off excess. Turn the potato cake in the bread crumbs. Gently shake off the excess. Place each breaded potato cake on the cookie sheet.

4. Heat 2 tablespoons of the oil in a large nonstick skillet over medium heat. Arrange 4 or 5 potato cakes in a single layer without crowding. Cook for 4 minutes, or until golden brown. Using 2 spatulas, carefully turn the potato cakes over and cook the other side for about 2 minutes, or until golden brown. Transfer the browned potato cakes to a platter. Add the remaining oil to the skillet and cook the remaining potato cakes.

Amalfitan~Style Mashed Potatoes

SERVES 6

Little bits of meatless bacon give these luscious mashed potatoes a wonderful smoky flavor, and soy milk makes the texture creamy smooth. Bake the potatoes in a casserole coated with bread crumbs and then serve up crunchy spoonfuls, just as my grandmother did for us.

6 medium baking potatoes
2 tablespoons extra virgin olive oil
3 strips meatless bacon, finely chopped
1 cup plain soy milk
1 medium yellow onion, finely chopped
1/4 cup coarsely chopped flat-leaf parsley
1/4 cup grated Romano cheese
   Salt and pepper to taste
1 cup plain bread crumbs

1. Peel the potatoes and cut each into quarters lengthwise, then cut each quarter in half. Place the potatoes in a bowl of cold water as you work to prevent them from turning brown. Drain the potatoes and place in a large pot with cold water to cover by 3 inches. Cover the pot and bring to a boil, then lower the heat to medium and cook the potatoes for about 12 minutes, or until soft when tested with a fork.

2. While the potatoes are cooking, heat the oil in a small skillet over medium heat. Add the meatless bacon, using a wooden spoon to separate the pieces. Cook, stirring frequently, for about 3 minutes, or until the bacon softens and releases some of its juices. Set aside until the potatoes are cooked.

3. Preheat the oven to 350 degrees. When the potatoes are cooked, reserve 1/2 cup of the cooking liquid, then drain the potatoes and return them to the pot.

4. Pour the reserved cooking liquid over the potatoes and mash them. Add the meatless bacon and the pan juices, using a rubber spatula to scrape out the pan. Add the soy milk, onion, parsley, 2 tablespoons of the cheese, and the salt and pepper. Continue mashing the potatoes until smooth and creamy. Taste for seasonings.

5. Spray a rectangular baking pan with olive oil cooking spray. Sprinkle 1/3 cup of the bread crumbs evenly over the bottom and sides of the pan, tilting the pan

to coat all sides. Turn the mashed potatoes into the prepared pan, using a rubber spatula to scrape out the pot and to smooth the potatoes evenly on top. Sprinkle the remaining 2 tablespoons of cheese evenly over the top, then sprinkle the remaining bread crumbs over the top. Bake for about 25 minutes, or until golden brown.

Roasted Potatoes with Rosemary and Garlic

SERVES 6

This dish goes beautifully with any entree—and wait until you smell the aroma in your kitchen!

6 **medium baking potatoes**
1 **large sweet onion, cut into 1/2-inch-wide ribs**
8 **large cloves garlic, unpeeled**
2 **tablespoons extra virgin olive oil**
2 **tablespoons fresh rosemary leaves**
   Salt and pepper to taste
1 **tablespoon water**

1. Preheat the oven to 425 degrees. Peel the potatoes and cut into quarters lengthwise. As you work, place the potatoes in a bowl of cold water to prevent them from turning brown. Drain the potatoes and place in a large bowl.

2. Scatter the onion and garlic cloves over the potatoes. Toss to mix. Drizzle the olive oil evenly over the vegetables, scatter the rosemary leaves on top, and sprinkle with salt and pepper. Add the water and toss thoroughly to mix.

3. Spray a large rimmed cookie sheet or jelly-roll pan with olive oil cooking spray. Turn the vegetables into the cookie sheet, using a rubber spatula to scrape the bowl of any juices. Spread the vegetables evenly. Bake for about 1 hour, or until the potatoes are golden brown and tender when tested with a fork.

Spiedini

SERVES 6

Spiedini is fresh mozzarella cheese (also known as fiore di latte, or "flower of milk"), encased in Italian bread, then sautéed in extra virgin olive oil with white wine, fresh lemon juice, and capers. Pair spiedini with a glass of Chianti Classico for a perfect appetizer or serve it as a side dish with Italian Hamburgers (page 191) and Sautéed Spinach (page 54).

Note: Buy a 10-inch round loaf of soft-crusted Italian bread from the bakery section of your supermarket and have it sliced.

> **5 to 6 (¹/₂-inch-thick) slices soft-crusted Italian bread**
> **¹/₄ cup extra virgin olive oil**
> **1 large clove garlic, minced**
> **1 pound fresh mozzarella cheese, drained (reserve liquid) and cut into 1-inch-thick slices**
> **2 tablespoons capers, drained**
> **Salt and pepper to taste**
> **3 tablespoons liquid from the mozzarella or milk**
> **3 tablespoons fresh lemon juice (about 1 lemon)**
> **3 tablespoons dry white wine**

1. Generously spray a 9 × 5-inch loaf pan with butter-flavored cooking spray. Arrange 4 or 5 slices of bread over the bottom and sides of the pan, trimming the bread to fit and overlapping slightly as needed.

2. In a small bowl, combine 2 tablespoons of the oil and the garlic. Brush the bread with the oil and garlic, then use a spoon to scatter any remaining garlic evenly on the bread.

3. Arrange the sliced mozzarella over the bread in the bottom of the loaf pan. Scatter 1 tablespoon of the capers evenly over the mozzarella. Sprinkle with salt and pepper, going light on the salt because the capers are a little salty. Using your hand or the back of a spoon, press the capers into the mozzarella. Cover the mozzarella with the remaining slice of bread and any bread trimmings. Sprinkle the 3 tablespoons of liquid from the mozzarella evenly over the bread. Sprinkle lightly with salt and pepper. Press and compact the loaf to about one-third of its original height. The liquid from the milk will make the bread soggy, which will make this step easy. Turn the loaf out onto a large plate. It should come out easily.

4. Heat the remaining 2 tablespoons of oil in a large nonstick skillet over medium heat. Add the remaining tablespoon of capers, the lemon juice, and wine. Sprinkle lightly with salt and pepper. Stir to mix. Carefully slide the loaf into the skillet, using a large plastic spatula to transfer the loaf. Cover and cook for 3 to 4 minutes, or until the mozzarella melts slightly and the bread is golden brown when you lift one edge. Carefully turn the loaf over to brown the other side. Cook for 2 to 3 minutes, or until the bread is golden brown.

5. Transfer the loaf to a large platter. Cut into six 1$\frac{1}{2}$-inch-thick slices. Serve immediately.

Friselle
(Little Pepper Nuggets)

MAKES ABOUT 50

Friselle are savory biscotti that are the perfect accompaniment to a glass of wine. They are ideal for a cocktail party, and in our family we munch on them during the afternoon for a snack. Friselle can be an elegant and luscious treat when served with strawberries drizzled lightly with a fine balsamic vinegar. The peppery flavor of the friselle complements the sweetness of the strawberries and makes a perfect foil for the sweet yet acidic flavor of the vinegar. Friselle will keep for weeks (if you can resist polishing them off in a couple of days) in a tightly covered tin. And they make a terrific gift when presented in an attractive jar or tin and accompanied by a good bottle of red wine.

> $3^1/_2$ **cups unbleached all-purpose flour**
> 1   **tablespoon black pepper, preferably freshly ground**
> 1   **teaspoon salt**
> 1   **tablespoon baking powder**
> $3/_4$ **cup olive oil**
> 1   **cup cold water**

1. Measure the flour, pepper, salt, and baking powder into a bowl. Stir well to combine. In a separate bowl, whisk the oil and water well to blend.

2. Pour the liquid over the dry ingredients all at once. Stir well to combine. The dough will be thick. Turn the dough onto a countertop and knead for 1 to 2 minutes, or until smooth. Roll the dough into a 14-inch-long cigar-shaped roll.

3. Preheat the oven to 350 degrees. Spray 2 or 3 cookie sheets with nonstick cooking spray. Cut the dough into 2-inch-thick slices. Roll each slice into a 13-inch-long pencil-shaped roll. Cut the rolls into 1-inch nuggets. Arrange the nuggets, cut side up, on the prepared cookie sheets, leaving $3/_4$ inch of space between them so they will bake evenly.

4. Bake for 1 hour 10 minutes, or until the friselle are golden brown and firm to the touch, rotating the cookie sheets after about 30 minutes for even baking. Let cool to room temperature before storing.

Stewed Red, Green, and Cubanelle Peppers

SERVES 6

Peppers are a rich source of vitamin C and fiber, and stewed peppers make a delicious, healthful side dish. They are also wonderful in a sandwich on Italian bread, which absorbs the flavorful juices. Cubanelle peppers (my mom refers to them as fryers) are long, plump, pale green peppers with a mild bell pepper flavor. They can be used in any recipe that calls for peppers.

> 2 **medium red bell peppers**
> 2 **medium green bell peppers**
> 2 **medium Cubanelle peppers**
> 3 **tablespoons olive oil**
> 1 **medium yellow onion, cut into thick ribs**
> 2 **large cloves garlic, cut into thick slices**
> 1 **ripe medium tomato, coarsely chopped, including juices**
> 1 **tablespoon chopped fresh oregano or 1 teaspoon dried**
>   **Salt and pepper to taste**

1. Cut the peppers in half lengthwise. Remove and discard the stems, seeds, and soft inner ribs. Rinse the peppers under cold water. Drain, cut side down, in a colander. Cut the pepper halves into thick ribs.

2. Heat the oil in a large pot over medium heat. Add the peppers, onion, garlic, tomato, oregano, salt, and pepper. Stir well to mix. Cook, stirring occasionally, for 20 minutes, or until the peppers are fork-tender. Taste for seasonings.

Sautéed Broccoli Rabe

SERVES 6

Broccoli rabe, also known as rapini or rabe, has grown in popularity, and I couldn't be happier because it's my favorite vegetable. At Claire's Corner Copia we can prepare this dish to suit the taste of different customers, but this recipe is one of my favorites. The broccoli is first cooked quickly in boiling water to remove some of the bitterness, then lightly sautéed in extra virgin olive oil with plenty of garlic and crushed red pepper flakes to give it a nice "zip." Use any leftovers for a sandwich made on Italian bread. Whether served plain or with a slice of provolone cheese, it's a sandwich you'll love.

2 large bunches broccoli rabe (about 2¼ pounds), bottom 2 inches of stem trimmed off, well washed
4 tablespoons extra virgin olive oil
4 large cloves garlic, cut into thick slivers
¼ teaspoon red pepper flakes
    Salt and pepper to taste
1 lemon, cut into 6 wedges (optional)

1. Bring a large pot of lightly salted water to a boil over high heat. Add the broccoli rabe, cover the pot, and cook at a boil for 5 minutes, using tongs occasionally to turn the broccoli rabe so that it will cook evenly. Drain the broccoli rabe in a colander.

2. Heat the oil in a large skillet over medium heat. Add the garlic and cook, stirring frequently, for 2 minutes, or until lightly browned but not burned.

3. Add the red pepper flakes and drained broccoli rabe. Sprinkle with salt and pepper. Cook for 3 to 4 minutes, or until tender to your preference, using tongs to turn the broccoli rabe occasionally to coat with oil and cook evenly. Taste for seasonings.

4. Turn out onto serving plates. Serve with lemon wedges for squeezing onto the broccoli rabe if desired. It adds a nice perky flavor and vitamin C too.

Fried Onion Slices

SERVES 6

In every family there is a dish each person finds irresistible. Fried onion slices is one of our favorites. Homemade fried onions beat any frozen variety, as I'm sure you'll agree after you've made a batch. Serve them with Sautéed Broccoli Rabe (page 39) and Italian Hamburgers (page 191), or if you want something quicker, just cook up store-bought veggie burgers.

3 **large sweet onions (Vidalia, Texas Sweet, or Walla Walla), cut into** **1/2-inch-thick slices but not separated into rings**
1/2 **cup unbleached all-purpose flour**
   Salt and pepper to taste
5 **eggs**
2 **tablespoons finely chopped flat-leaf parsley**
2 **cups plain dry bread crumbs**
1/2 **cup olive oil**

1. Arrange the slices of onion in a single layer on 2 cookie sheets. Measure the flour into a shallow bowl. Season with salt and pepper.

2. Beat the eggs in a medium bowl. Stir in the parsley and a little salt and pepper.

3. Measure the bread crumbs into a separate shallow bowl. Line a second cookie sheet with a double layer of paper towels and set it by the stove.

4. Carefully lift 1 slice of onion and dredge it in the seasoned flour. Gently shake off the excess. Dip the onion slice into the egg, coating both sides. Shake off the excess. Turn the onion slice in the bread crumbs, covering both sides with crumbs. Return the breaded onion slice to the cookie sheet and repeat the process until all the onion slices are breaded.

5. Heat 1/4 cup of the oil in a large nonstick skillet over medium heat. Carefully lower 5 or 6 breaded onion rings into the heated oil (do not overcrowd or the oil temperature will drop and the onion slices will be greasy). Fry each side for about 2 minutes, or until golden brown. It's easier to turn the onion slices if you use 2 slotted spatulas. Transfer the browned onion slices to the towel-lined cookie sheet. Continue frying the onion slices, adding more oil as needed. Serve immediately or at room temperature.

Marinated Mushrooms

SERVES 4 TO 6

No antipasto course is complete in our house without marinated vegetables, particularly marinated eggplant or mushrooms. Marinated mushrooms are also delicious in a tossed salad or on a sandwich. In fact, a sandwich of marinated mushrooms and sliced provolone cheese on Italian bread is simply delicious. Prepare a batch of these mushrooms and keep them in your refrigerator for a few weeks—that is, if you can resist them for that long.

1 **pound small to medium mushrooms**
2 **quarts water**
2 **quarts white vinegar**
1 **rib celery, finely chopped**
2 **tablespoons extra virgin olive oil**
3 **large cloves garlic, coarsely chopped**
1 **teaspoon dried oregano**
1/2 **teaspoon red pepper flakes**
   Salt and pepper to taste

1. Rinse and drain the mushrooms. Cut off and discard a thin slice from the bottom of each stem.

2. Bring the water and vinegar to boil in a large stainless-steel pot. Add the mushrooms, cover, and cook for 4 minutes, or until the mushrooms are fork-tender. Drain in a colander.

3. Turn the drained mushrooms into a bowl. Add the celery, oil, garlic, oregano, red pepper flakes, salt, and pepper. Toss to mix thoroughly. Taste for seasonings. Turn into a clean jar with a tight-fitting lid or into a clean bowl. Allow to cool to room temperature.

4. Although these mushrooms are delicious and ready to eat immediately, the flavors continue to improve as the mushrooms marinate in the olive oil and herbs. Cover and refrigerate for up to 1 month.

Marinated Olives

MAKES ABOUT 85 OLIVES

I like to keep a little jar of these marinated olives in my refrigerator for unexpected company. I serve them with crostini, the little toasted slices of Italian bread that I always keep on hand, and perhaps some pieces of Parmigiano-Reggiano cheese. Just open a bottle of good Chianti, and your guests will be pleasantly satisfied.

   1   **pound assorted olives (oil-cured, large black, small green), drained**
   2   **tablespoons extra virgin olive oil**
   1   **tablespoon fresh rosemary leaves or 1 teaspoon dried**
   1   **tablespoon chopped fresh oregano or 1 teaspoon dried**
2$^1/_2$ **teaspoons fresh thyme leaves or $^1/_2$ teaspoon dried**
       Freshly ground black pepper to taste

Place all the ingredients in a bowl and stir to mix. Taste for seasonings. Spoon into a large jar with a wide mouth and refrigerate until needed. Stir to mix each time before serving.

Artichokes Baked with Asiago Cheese

SERVES 6

We serve this as a side dish with Vegetarian Meat Loaf (page 192) or pasta with Basil-Scented Marinara Sauce (page 150). It also makes a luscious sandwich filling on Italian bread. Asiago cheese is a semi-firm Italian cheese with a delicious creamy, nutty flavor.

2 (14-ounce) cans artichoke hearts, drained, cut in half lengthwise
6 large green olives, pitted and chopped
3 large cloves garlic, finely chopped
1 rib celery, finely chopped
1/4 cup coarsely chopped flat-leaf parsley
2 tablespoons extra virgin olive oil
3 tablespoons fresh lemon juice (about 1 lemon)
1 tablespoon finely chopped fresh mint or 1 teaspoon dried
   Salt and pepper to taste
4 ounces Asiago cheese, coarsely grated

1. Preheat the oven to 375 degrees. Place the artichoke hearts, olives, garlic, celery, and parsley in a bowl. Toss to mix. Add the oil, lemon juice, mint, salt, and pepper. Toss to combine and coat evenly. Taste for seasonings.

2. Spray a 2-quart glass casserole dish with nonstick cooking spray. Turn the artichoke mixture into the prepared dish, using a rubber spatula to scrape the bowl of its juices. Sprinkle the cheese evenly over the artichokes. Bake for 25 minutes, or until the cheese is melted and the artichokes are heated through.

Beets and Potatoes with Carrots

SERVES 6

This is an especially colorful vegetable combination. Any leftovers are delicious served chilled the next day.

3 large beets (about 1 pound), peeled and cut into 6 wedges
4 medium carrots, peeled and cut into $1/2$-inch-thick slices
5 medium boiling potatoes, peeled and cut into 8 wedges
1 small yellow onion, cut into thin slices and separated into rings
2 large cloves garlic, finely chopped
3 tablespoons extra virgin olive oil
$1/4$ cup red wine vinegar
   Salt and pepper to taste

1. Bring a large pot of lightly salted water to a boil over high heat. Add the beets, carrots, and potatoes. Cook, uncovered, stirring occasionally, for about 20 minutes, or until the beets are tender. Drain and turn into a bowl.

2. Add the onion and garlic. Toss to mix. Drizzle the olive oil and vinegar over the vegetables. Add salt and pepper and toss well to mix. Taste for seasonings.

Sautéed Carrots with Onions and Green Peas

SERVES 4

You can serve this colorful side dish with any entree, but I especially like it with Roasted-Garlic Mashed Potatoes (page 30) and Porcini Mushroom Gravy (page 49) and Stuffed Portobello Mushrooms (page 187).

1½ tablespoons extra virgin olive oil
1 large yellow onion, cut into thick ribs
1 medium leek, white and pale green parts only, well washed and coarsely chopped
5 medium carrots, peeled and cut into ¼-inch-thick diagonal slices
Salt and pepper to taste
1 cup frozen green peas, thawed
2 tablespoons finely chopped fresh mint or 1 teaspoon dried

Heat the oil in a large skillet over low heat. Add the onion, leek, carrots, salt, and pepper. Cover and cook, stirring occasionally, for 10 minutes, or until the carrots are tender. Stir in the peas. Cover and continue cooking for 1 minute, stirring occasionally. Taste for seasonings.

Sautéed Mushrooms

SERVES 4

Sauté your favorite combination of mushrooms and serve them as a side dish, in a sandwich on Italian bread with a slice of provolone cheese, or with Sautéed Endive (page 52) and Sautéed Radicchio (page 53) for a lovely antipasto platter.

2 tablespoons extra virgin olive oil
2 large cloves garlic, thinly sliced
1 pound assorted mushrooms (button, shiitake, oyster, and portobello), cut into thick slices
  Salt and pepper to taste
2 tablespoons balsamic vinegar
2 tablespoons finely chopped flat-leaf parsley

1. Heat the oil in a large skillet over medium heat. Add the garlic, mushrooms, salt, and pepper. Cover and cook, stirring occasionally, for about 5 minutes, or until the mushrooms are just tender.

2. Drizzle the vinegar evenly over the mushrooms and stir in. Cook, uncovered, for 1 minute. Using a slotted spoon, transfer the mushrooms to a platter. Scatter the parsley evenly over the mushrooms.

Mushrooms with Lemon, White Wine, and Parsley

SERVES 6

This side dish is also delicious over pappardelle pasta. Use any combination of your favorite mushrooms for this dish.

2 tablespoons extra virgin olive oil
1 large shallot, finely chopped
1 large clove garlic, cut into thin slices
1 pound assorted mushrooms (button, cremini, portobello, and shiitake), cut into 1/4-inch-thick slices
   Salt and pepper to taste
3 tablespoons fresh lemon juice (about 1 lemon)
3 tablespoons dry white wine
1/4 cup finely chopped flat-leaf parsley

1. Heat the oil in a large skillet over medium heat. Add the shallot, garlic, mushrooms, salt, and pepper. Cook, stirring occasionally, for about 7 minutes, or until the mushrooms are crisp-tender.

2. Add the lemon juice, wine, and parsley. Continue cooking, stirring occasionally, for 7 minutes, or until the mushrooms are tender and most of the liquids have evaporated. Taste for seasonings.

Roasted Portobello Mushrooms with Mint and Garlic

SERVES 4

The aromatic combination of mint and garlic is a perfect match for meaty portobello mushrooms. Team them with Amalfitan-Style Mashed Potatoes (page 32) and Sauté of Zucchini, Plum Tomatoes, and Sweet Onion (page 22) for a wonderful meal.

8 medium portobello mushroom caps (about 12 ounces), rinsed and drained
2 tablespoons extra virgin olive oil
3 tablespoons finely chopped fresh mint or 1 tablespoon dried
4 large cloves garlic, finely chopped
3 tablespoons fresh lemon juice (about 1 lemon)
Salt and pepper to taste

1. Preheat the oven to 350 degrees. Place the mushroom caps in a large bowl. Drizzle the oil evenly over the mushroom caps and toss gently with your hands to coat them well. Scatter the mint, garlic, and lemon juice over the mushroom caps, sprinkle with salt and pepper, and toss gently to combine.

2. Spray a 13 × 9-inch glass baking dish with olive oil cooking spray. Arrange the mushroom caps, stem side down, in a single layer in the pan. Use a rubber spatula to scrape out the bowl, distributing the mint, garlic, and juices evenly over the mushrooms.

3. Pour 1/4 cup water into the pan, around, not over, the mushroom caps. Cover the pan tightly with foil. Bake for 30 minutes, then remove the foil and continue baking for 15 minutes, or until the mushrooms are just tender when tested with a fork.

Porcini Mushroom Gravy

MAKES ABOUT 3¼ CUPS

Dried porcini mushrooms have a rich, earthy flavor and a pleasant, chewy texture (once they are reconstituted), and they are readily available in most supermarkets. Fresh porcini mushrooms have an equally rich flavor and an incredible meaty texture, but unless you visit Italy either in the late spring or during the fall, you are unlikely to find them. If you are lucky enough to discover fresh porcini in your market, expect to pay a small fortune for them. For now most of us must be satisfied with the dried mushrooms, which impart a wonderful, woodsy flavor to soups, sauces, and gravy.

$^1/_2$ **ounce dried porcini mushrooms**
2 **cups hot tap water**
2 **tablespoons butter or soybean margarine**
1 **large clove garlic, finely chopped**
1 **medium yellow onion, finely chopped**
3 **tablespoons unbleached all-purpose flour**
1 **cup milk or soy milk**
1 **tablespoon Marsala wine**
   Salt and pepper to taste

1. Place the dried mushrooms in a large bowl, pour the hot tap water over them, and allow them to soften for about 20 minutes. Using your hands, gently rub each mushroom and swish the mushrooms around in the water to remove any grit. Allow them to rest for 10 minutes so the grit will sink to the bottom of the bowl.

2. Using a slotted spoon, lift out the mushrooms so that the grit remains at the bottom. Strain the soaking water through a fine-mesh strainer set over a bowl and reserve it. Finely chop the mushrooms

3. Heat the butter in a large skillet over medium-low heat. Add the chopped mushrooms, garlic, and onion. Cover and cook, stirring occasionally, for 5 minutes, or until the onion has softened. Sprinkle the flour evenly over the vegetables. Stir well to mix. Cook, uncovered, for about 2 minutes, stirring frequently.

4. Add the reserved soaking water, milk, Marsala, salt, and pepper. Stir well to combine. Raise the heat to medium and bring the liquid to a boil, stirring frequently. Cook at a medium boil, stirring frequently, for 8 to 10 minutes, or until the mixture thickens. Taste for seasonings.

Stewed Leeks and Tomatoes with White Wine

SERVES 4

This side dish also makes a delicious sauce for polenta or angel hair pasta. Leeks look like big scallions and have a mild and pleasant onion-garlic flavor. They release a delightful fragrance when sautéed. Keep in mind that leeks can be quite gritty and the grit is often trapped in between the layers that all onions have. When I prepare leeks for a recipe, I first cut them, then soak them in plenty of cool water, swishing the water to loosen any grit. Then, using my hands, I lift out the leeks, leaving the grit behind. Repeat the process until no grit remains in the water.

 3 tablespoons extra virgin olive oil
 2 medium leeks, white and pale green parts only, coarsely chopped
 2 ripe large tomatoes, coarsely chopped, including juices
 1/4 cup dry white wine
 5 large fresh basil leaves
   Salt and pepper to taste

Heat the oil in a large skillet over medium heat. Add the leeks, tomatoes, wine, basil, salt, and pepper. Stir to mix. Cook, stirring occasionally, for 10 minutes, or until the tomatoes are soft and the leeks are crisp-tender. Taste for seasonings.

Sautéed Fennel

SERVES 4

Fennel, also called finocchio (*pronounced fee-NO-kee-o*), *looks like celery with a bulbous body and feathery leaves. It is delicious eaten raw in a salad, roasted, grilled, or sautéed. In my family we often cut it into sticks and eat it raw, the way most people eat carrots or apples.*

2 **tablespoons extra virgin olive oil**
1 **large head fennel, bottom** 1/2 **inch trimmed off, cut lengthwise into** 1/2**-inch pieces**
Salt and pepper to taste
2 **tablespoons fresh lemon juice (about** 1/2 **lemon)**
2 **tablespoons finely chopped flat-leaf parsley**

1. Heat the oil in a large skillet over medium-low heat. Add the fennel, salt, and pepper. Cover and cook for about 10 minutes, or until the fennel is fork-tender, using tongs to turn the fennel occasionally. Taste for seasonings.

2. Turn out into a serving dish, using a rubber spatula to scrape the skillet of any juices. Drizzle the lemon juice and scatter the parsley evenly over the fennel.

Sautéed Endive

SERVES 4

Belgian endive is so versatile. You can chop the long cigar-shaped leaves and add them to a tossed salad for an interesting touch, or stuff the leaves with fillings to make appetizers. Sautéed Belgian endive is an elegant-looking side dish. Serve it with Sautéed Radicchio (page 53) and Sautéed Mushrooms (page 46) for a beautiful antipasto platter.

2½ tablespoons extra virgin olive oil
2 large Belgian endives, cut in half lengthwise
Salt and pepper to taste
2 tablespoons dry white wine

1. Heat the oil in a large skillet over medium-low heat. Add the endives, cut side down, and the salt and pepper. Cover and cook for 8 to 10 minutes or until the endives wilt and the undersides are a celery color.

2. Carefully turn the endives over and sprinkle with salt and pepper. Cover and cook for 5 minutes, or until the undersides are a celery color.

3. Drizzle the wine evenly over the endives. Cook, uncovered, for 1 minute. Turn out onto a platter and spoon the pan juices over the tops.

Sautéed Radicchio

SERVES 4

For a beautiful color combination, sauté thick chunks of dark red heads of radicchio (pronounced ra-DEE-kee-o) and serve them on a platter with Sautéed Endive (page 52) and Sautéed Mushrooms (page 46). The sautéed radicchio is scrumptious in a sandwich on Italian bread with maybe a slice of provolone cheese.

3 tablespoons extra virgin olive oil
2 large cloves garlic, thinly sliced
1 large head radicchio, cut lengthwise into 6 wedges
　Salt and pepper to taste
1 tablespoon fresh lemon juice (about $1/2$ lemon)

Heat the oil in a large skillet over medium heat. Add the garlic, radicchio, salt, and pepper. Cover and cook, stirring occasionally, for about 5 minutes, or until the radicchio is just tender and wilted. Turn out onto a platter. Drizzle the lemon juice evenly over the radicchio.

Sautéed Spinach

SERVES 4

Both my mom and my grandmother served spinach a few times a week, either as a side dish or in soup. My grandmother used this recipe, and she always served lemon wedges on the side to perk up the taste.

> 1   **10-ounce bag fresh spinach**
> 2   **tablespoons extra virgin olive oil**
> 3   **large cloves garlic, cut into thin slices**
>   **Salt and pepper to taste**
> 1/2 **lemon, cut into 4 wedges**

1. Trim off only the thick spinach stems, leaving the thin stems intact. Wash the spinach thoroughly to remove any grit, then drain in a colander for a few minutes. Place the spinach with the water still clinging to its leaves in a large skillet over medium heat. Cook, uncovered, for 5 to 6 minutes, or until the spinach is just wilted, using tongs to turn the spinach occasionally. Drain in a colander.

2. Carefully wipe the skillet dry with paper towels. Heat the oil in the skillet over medium heat. Add the garlic and cook, stirring occasionally, for 2 minutes, or until it is golden brown but not burned. Add the drained spinach, salt, and pepper. Cook, stirring, for 1 minute, or until the spinach is tender and completely coated with oil. Turn into a serving dish and arrange the lemon wedges around the edge.

Sun~Dried Tomato Muffins

MAKES 12 MUFFINS

These flavorful muffins are the perfect accompaniment to a nice bowl of soup or a salad for a light supper.

2 cups unbleached all-purpose flour
1/3 cup grated Parmigiano-Reggiano cheese
1 tablespoon baking powder
1/2 teaspoon dried oregano
1/4 teaspoon salt
1/4 teaspoon pepper
1 egg
1 cup milk or soy milk
3 tablespoons olive oil
1/4 cup drained and finely chopped sun-dried tomatoes in oil
2 tablespoons finely chopped yellow onion
2 tablespoons finely chopped flat-leaf parsley

1. Preheat the oven to 375 degrees. Measure the flour, cheese, baking powder, oregano, salt, and pepper into a large bowl. Stir to mix.

2. In a separate bowl, combine the egg, milk, oil, sun-dried tomatoes, onion, and parsley. Whisk well to mix. Pour over the dry ingredients. Stir to combine but don't beat the batter or the muffins will be tough.

3. Spray a muffin tin with nonstick cooking spray. Fill each cup two-thirds full with batter. Bake for about 20 minutes, or until the muffins are golden brown and a tester comes out clean when inserted into the center of a muffin. Serve warm or at room temperature.

Onion~Parmesan Puffs

MAKES 20 LARGE OR 30 APPETIZER-SIZE PUFFS

The batter for these tasty treats is made like the Cream Puff (page 233) batter because it, too, is a choux pastry. You can serve these light little gems as part of your appetizer selection with cocktails, or you can make them larger and fill with warmed Porcini Mushroom Gravy (page 49) for a lovely entree. You can also use these puffs as sandwich bread. They will liven up even plain tomato sandwiches.

1 **cup water**
1/2 **cup butter (1 stick) or vegetable shortening**
1 **small onion, finely chopped**
1 **tablespoon finely chopped flat-leaf parsley**
   Salt and pepper to taste
1 **cup unbleached all-purpose flour**
1/2 **cup grated Parmigiano-Reggiano cheese**
4 **eggs**

1. Preheat the oven to 400 degrees. Spray 2 cookie sheets with nonstick cooking spray. Bring the water, butter, onion, and parsley to a boil in a large pot over high heat, stirring occasionally until the butter melts.

2. Add the salt and pepper, then add the flour all at once. Stir with a spoon to mix, then beat for about 2 minutes, or until the mixture is thick and smooth and pulls away from the pan. Beat in the grated cheese.

3. Remove the pot from the stove and continue beating for a minute to cool the mixture slightly. Add 1 egg and beat vigorously for about 1 minute, or until the mixture is smooth. Add the remaining eggs, one at a time, beating for 1 minute after each addition, until the mixture is smooth.

4. For appetizer-size puffs, drop the mixture by heaping teaspoons onto the cookie sheets. Bake for about 30 minutes, or until the puffs are medium golden brown.

5. For larger puffs to use as sandwich bread, drop the mixture by heaping tablespoons onto the cookie sheets, leaving 2 inches between them. Bake for about 35 minutes, or until the puffs are medium golden brown.

Cipolline Fritte
(Fried Little Onions)

SERVES 6

Cipolline are sold in supermarkets across the country during the fall. They come mainly from Verona, Italy, and resemble a small and somewhat flat-shaped Vidalia onion with a sweet yet strong onion flavor. Although cipolline are really the bulb of the grape hyacinth plant, we continue to refer to them as little onions.

24 **medium cipolline, peeled**
  Salt and pepper to taste
2 **cups all-purpose flour**
2 **teaspoons baking powder**
2 **eggs**
1 **cup water**
2 **tablespoons finely chopped flat-leaf parsley**
1 **cup sunflower or peanut oil**

1. Bring 2 quarts of water to a boil in a large pot over high heat. Add the cipolline and a little salt. Cover and cook for about 3 minutes, or until fork-tender. Drain.

2. Measure the flour, baking powder, salt, and pepper into a bowl. Combine the eggs, water, salt, and pepper in a separate bowl. Whisk well to blend. Stir this mixture into the flour mixture. Stir in the parsley, mixing well to blend.

3. Cover a cookie sheet with a double layer of paper towels and place it next to the stove. Heat the oil in a large, deep skillet over medium-high heat. When it is hot (test by dropping a pinch of batter into the hot oil; if it sizzles and rises quickly, the oil is ready), dip a cipolline into the batter to coat. Gently shake off the excess. Drop the batter-coated cipolline into the hot oil. Working quickly, repeat the process with 5 or 6 more cipolline. Do not crowd the pot or the temperature of the oil will drop and make the cipolline greasy.

4. Cook for about 2 minutes, or until the cipolline are golden brown. Using tongs, turn the cipolline and cook the other side for about 2 minutes. Using a strainer or slotted spoon, lift the cooked cipolline out of the oil, holding the strainer over the pot, for a few seconds to allow the cipolline to drain. Transfer the fried cipolline to the towel-lined cookie sheet. Continue frying the cipolline in batches. Serve hot or at room temperature.

Peas and Cipolline with Meatless Bacon

SERVES 6

During my visits to southern Italy, I came across many restaurant menus that offered this dish made with pancetta, a sugar- and salt-cured Italian bacon. There are many brands of meatless bacon available in supermarkets and health foods stores, and they will add a meaty flavor to this dish while providing good-quality vegetable protein.

Note: You can find cipolline, the sharp-sweet little Italian onions (actually the bulbs of the grape hyacinth), in most supermarkets.

12	**cipolline, unpeeled**
2	**tablespoons olive oil**
1	**large shallot, finely chopped**
4	**strips meatless bacon, coarsely chopped**
	Salt and pepper to taste
1/4	**cup dry white wine**
2	**cups frozen tiny green peas, thawed**

1. Bring 1 quart of lightly salted water to a boil in a medium pot over high heat. Add the cipolline, cover, and cook for about 5 minutes, or until crisp-tender. Drain. When cool enough to handle, peel the skins from the onions.

2. Heat the oil in a large skillet over medium heat. Add the shallot, bacon, salt, and pepper. Cover and cook, stirring occasionally, for 4 to 5 minutes, or until the shallot is softened.

3. Add the wine and the cipolline. Stir to mix. Cover and cook for 3 to 5 minutes, or until the cipolline are tender.

4. Stir in the peas, cover, and cook for 2 to 3 minutes, or until heated through. Taste for seasonings.

Chickpeas with Tomatoes and Rosemary

SERVES 4

This protein- and fiber-packed side dish can be prepared using canned chickpeas for convenience. I like to keep a can of organic chickpeas, sold in health foods stores, on hand for this dish. You can also toss this mixture with your favorite cooked pasta for a quick entree; when chilled, it makes a terrific pasta salad.

1   **(15-ounce) can chickpeas, drained**
1   **pint ripe cherry tomatoes, cut into halves**
1   **large clove garlic, finely chopped**
2   **tablespoons extra virgin olive oil**
1   **tablespoon fresh rosemary leaves or 1 teaspoon dried**
2   **tablespoons finely chopped fresh mint or 1 teaspoon dried**
    Salt and pepper to taste

Combine the ingredients in a bowl and toss well. Taste for seasonings.

Green Beans Stewed with Tomatoes

SERVES 6

Sometimes I eat just a bowl of these "string beans" for supper, using crusty Italian bread to sop up the luscious juices.

3 tablespoons extra virgin olive oil
3 large cloves garlic, finely chopped
1 large yellow onion, cut into thick ribs
12 ounces green beans, trimmed and cut in half
1 ripe large tomato, coarsely chopped, including juices
Salt and pepper to taste
1 (6-ounce) can tomato paste
3 cups water
5 large fresh basil leaves, coarsely chopped
1/8 teaspoon ground cloves
1/8 teaspoon ground red pepper

1. Heat the oil in a large pot over medium heat. Add the garlic, onion, green beans, tomato, salt, and pepper. Stir well to coat with the oil. Cover and cook, stirring occasionally, for 10 minutes, or until the vegetables have softened and released some of their juices.

2. Add the tomato paste, water, basil, cloves, and red pepper. Stir well to mix thoroughly. Cover and bring to a medium-high boil. Cook, stirring occasionally, for 15 to 20 minutes, or until the green beans are tender. Taste for seasonings.

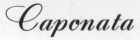 Caponata

SERVES 6

Although in our family caponata is served as an appetizer, it is filling enough to be an entree. Or you can toss it with angel hair pasta or use it as a sandwich filling. Hot or chilled, it is a delicious eggplant stew.

1/4 **cup olive oil**
1 **large yellow onion, coarsely chopped**
1 **large clove garlic, finely chopped**
3 **medium eggplants (about 2**1/4 **pounds), unpeeled, cut into 1-inch cubes**
3 **ribs celery, cut into** 1/4**-inch-thick slices**
   Salt and pepper to taste
1 **(6-ounce) can tomato paste**
2 **tablespoons pine nuts**
2 **cups water**
2 **tablespoons capers, drained**
1/4 **cup sliced green olives**
1/4 **cup red wine vinegar**
2 **tablespoons sugar**

1. Heat the oil in a large pot over medium-low heat. Add the onion, garlic, eggplants, celery, salt, and pepper. Cover and cook, stirring occasionally, for about 25 minutes, or until the eggplant is barely tender and has released some of its juices.

2. Add the tomato paste, pine nuts, and water. Stir well to blend. Cover and cook, stirring frequently, for about 20 minutes, or until the eggplant is very tender.

3. Add the capers, olives, vinegar, and sugar. Stir well to combine. Cover and cook for 3 minutes, stirring frequently. Taste for seasonings.

Sautéed Eggplant

SERVES 6

Eggplant has always been a staple in the southern Italian diet, but over the years it has become wildly popular in my restaurant too. You can serve this fiber-rich sauté as a side dish or a delicious sandwich filling, or spoon it over your favorite pasta. Try making it with purple Sicilian eggplants or creamy white eggplants.

2 **medium eggplants (about 1¹/₂ pounds), unpeeled, cut into 1-inch cubes**
  Salt and pepper to taste
3 **tablespoons extra virgin olive oil**
1 **medium yellow onion, cut into thick ribs**
2 **large cloves garlic, coarsely chopped**
1 **ripe large tomato, coarsely chopped**
10 **large fresh basil leaves**
¹/₄ **cup dry red wine**

1. Place the eggplant in a bowl. Add the salt and pepper and toss well. Set aside for 10 minutes.

2. Heat the oil in a large skillet over medium heat. Add the onion, garlic, tomato, basil, salt, and pepper. Using your hands, lift some of the eggplant from the bowl and squeeze gently to remove some of the liquid. Add the eggplant to the skillet. Continue to squeeze handfuls of the remaining eggplant and add to the skillet. Stir to coat with the oil.

3. Cover and cook, stirring occasionally, for 10 to 12 minutes, or until the eggplant is just tender. Add the wine. Stir to mix. Cover and continue cooking for 2 to 3 minutes, or until the eggplant is soft. Taste for seasonings.

Grilled Eggplant Slices

SERVES 4

If you have a grill-type pan, one with ridges that will produce the lines of an outdoor grill, use it for this recipe. If not, use a plain skillet. Grilled eggplant slices are a good addition to an antipasto platter, and they are excellent in a sandwich on Italian bread, drizzled with a little Pesto Vinaigrette (page 111).

> **2 medium white eggplants (about 1¹/₂ pounds)**
> **Salt and pepper to taste**
> **1 tablespoon olive oil**

1. Trim the ends from the eggplants but do not peel them. Cut the eggplants lengthwise into ¹/₄-inch-thick slices. Sprinkle the slices with salt and pepper and stack them on a platter.

2. Heat a large nonstick skillet over medium-high heat. Brush the skillet with about 1 teaspoon of olive oil. Arrange as many slices as will fit in a single layer in the skillet. Cook the eggplant for 3 to 4 minutes, or until it is medium brown (but not burned) and fork-tender. Turn the slices and cook the other side for 2 to 3 minutes, or until medium brown and fork-tender.

3. Transfer the cooked eggplant slices to a platter, overlapping slightly. Repeat with the remaining eggplant slices.

Soups, Salads, Dressings, and Sandwiches

Vegetable Soup with Pastina
Tomato Soup with Arborio Rice and Basil
Minestra
Ribollita
Zuppa Pavese
Tomato and Cabbage Soup
Lentil Soup
Fresh Tomato Soup with Garlic Toasts
Pasta e Fagioli
Lentil and Sausage Soup
Vegetable Soup with Chicory and Escarole
Split Pea Soup with Meatless Hot Dogs
Minestrone
Chickpea and Tomato Soup with Pasta Shells
Fennel Salad
Italian Potato Salad
Salad from Sorrento
Mushroom Salad with Celery and Parmigiano Curls
Broccoli and Potato Salad with Green Sauce
White Bean and Mint Salad
Red Oak Lettuce, Pears, Walnuts, and Gorgonzola in Lime Vinaigrette

Sausage Salad with Arugula and Tomatoes
Panzanella (Bread and Vegetable Salad)
Broccoli Salad
Green Bean and Tomato Salad
Salad from Capri
Bacon, Arugula, and Tomato on Italian Bread with Basil Mayonnaise
Salad of Oranges, Red Onions, and Oil-Cured Black Olives
"Beef" Salad
Sun-Dried Tomato Vinaigrette
Italian Dressing
Lemon-Mint Vinaigrette
Creamy Garlic Dressing
Red Wine Vinaigrette
Pesto Vinaigrette

Vegetable Soup with Pastina

SERVES 8

The tiny little dots of pasta called pastina are wonderful in soups, with butter and eggs (page 136), and with a simple marinara sauce. Freshly grated Parmigiana-Reggiano cheese on top gives pastina a special zest. In our family babies ate pastina as one of their first foods. (Don't laugh, but my mom always gave pastina with eggs and butter to our dogs while they were puppies.) It is one of the healthiest basic staples of the southern Italian kitchen.

Note: Ronzoni is one of only a few companies that make pastina, and it is very good.

   4 **tablespoons butter or soybean margarine ($^1/_2$ stick), cut into thick slices**
   1 **large yellow onion, coarsely chopped**
   6 **medium carrots, peeled and diced**
   6 **ribs celery, finely chopped**
   2 **large parsnips, peeled and diced**
$^1/_2$ **cup finely chopped flat-leaf parsley**
      Salt and pepper to taste
   1 **(35-ounce) can Italian whole peeled tomatoes in juice, squeezed with your hands to crush**
   2 **quarts water**
   3 **large baking potatoes, peeled and cut into small pieces**
   2 **cups corn kernels, preferably freshly cut from 2 ears corn**
   1 **large bay leaf**
  10 **large fresh basil leaves**
   2 **medium zucchini, diced**
   1 **(10-ounce) bag spinach, washed and finely chopped**
$^1/_2$ **cup pastina**

   1. Melt the butter in a large soup pot over medium-low heat. Add the onion, carrots, celery, parsnips, parsley, salt, and pepper. Cover and cook, stirring occasionally, for 20 minutes, or until the vegetables have released some of their moisture.
   2. Add the tomatoes and water. Stir well to combine. Raise the heat to high and

bring to a boil (this will take about 10 minutes). Lower the heat to medium, cover, and cook at a medium boil, stirring occasionally, for 30 minutes. Add the potatoes, corn, bay leaf, basil, zucchini, and spinach. Stir to combine. Cover and continue cooking at a medium boil, stirring occasionally, for about 15 minutes, or until the potatoes are just tender.

3. Stir in the pastina. Cover and continue cooking, stirring occasionally, for about 5 minutes, or until the pastina is tender. Taste for seasonings.

Tomato Soup with Arborio Rice and Basil

SERVES 8

Prepare this soup with San Marzano tomatoes, imported from Italy, for the best possible flavor.

3 tablespoons extra virgin olive oil
3 large cloves garlic, coarsely chopped
1 large shallot, finely chopped
1 large sweet onion, finely chopped
2 (35-ounce) cans whole peeled tomatoes in juice, squeezed with your hands to crush
2 quarts water
1/4 cup coarsely chopped flat-leaf parsley
10 large fresh basil leaves, coarsely chopped
2 bay leaves
Salt and pepper to taste
1 cup Arborio rice (Italian risotto rice)
1/2 cup dry white wine

1. Heat the oil in a large pot over medium-low heat. Add the garlic, shallot, and onion. Cover and cook, stirring occasionally, for 5 minutes, or until the onion has softened.

2. Add the tomatoes, water, parsley, basil, bay leaves, salt, and pepper. Raise the heat to high, cover, and bring to a boil. Lower the heat to medium and cook at a medium boil, stirring occasionally, for 1 hour 20 minutes.

3. Stir in the rice and wine. Cover and continue cooking at a medium boil, stirring frequently, for 20 minutes, or until the rice is tender. Taste for seasonings.

Minestra

SERVES 8 TO 10

Minestra *means "soup" in Italian, but this particular minestra was always reserved for Easter Sunday. It is a bountiful holiday soup made with white beans, an abundance of escarole, a little tomato, and the rich Italian dried salami known as pepperoni. Yves brand makes a meatless pepperoni with superb flavor. You can find it in health foods stores and some supermarkets.*

> 4 quarts water
> 1 pound dried cannellini, picked over
> 1 bay leaf
> 1/4 cup olive oil
> 2 tablespoons butter or soybean margarine
> 5 large cloves garlic, coarsely chopped
> 1/4 cup finely chopped flat-leaf parsley
> 3 tablespoons tomato paste
> 3 large heads escarole, well washed, cut into 2-inch pieces
> Salt and pepper to taste
> 1/2 teaspoon red pepper flakes
> 3 medium baking potatoes, peeled and cut into 1-inch pieces
> 1 (5 1/2-ounce) package meatless pepperoni, coarsely chopped

1. Place the water, cannellini, and bay leaf in a stockpot. Cover and bring to a boil over high heat. Lower the heat to medium and cook, covered, at a medium boil for 45 minutes, stirring occasionally.

2. Add the oil, butter, garlic, parsley, and tomato paste. Cover and cook, stirring occasionally, for 45 minutes, or until the beans are barely tender.

3. Add the escarole, salt, pepper, red pepper flakes, and potatoes. Stir well to mix. Cover and return to a boil (this should take about 15 minutes). Lower the heat to medium and cook at a medium boil, stirring occasionally, for 30 to 45 minutes, or until the beans are very tender. Stir in the pepperoni. Cover and continue cooking for 2 minutes, stirring occasionally. Taste for seasonings.

 Ribollita

SERVES 8 TO 10

Ribollita is a white bean and vegetable soup that is baked with toasted bread. When in Italy, I eat it nearly every day. In our family we make a version of this soup that we call pane cotta *and cook the bread with the soup on top of the stove. Either way, it's chock full of delicious, healthful ingredients.*

  4 **quarts water**
  8 **ounces dried cannellini, picked over (about 1 cup)**
  4 **large cloves garlic, finely chopped**
  1 **large yellow onion, cut into thick ribs**
  1/2 **cup coarsely chopped flat-leaf parsley**
  1 **large bay leaf**
  1/2 **teaspoon red pepper flakes**
  5 **tablespoons extra virgin olive oil**
  3 **carrots, peeled and cut into 1/4-inch-thick slices**
  3 **ribs celery, cut into 1/4-inch-thick slices**
  1/4 **head cauliflower, coarsely chopped**
  1/4 **head green cabbage, coarsely chopped**
  1 **ripe large tomato, finely chopped, including juices**
  1 **tablespoon chopped fresh oregano or 1 teaspoon dried**
  1 **teaspoon fennel seeds**
    Salt and pepper to taste
  1 **head escarole, washed thoroughly and coarsely chopped**
 10 **(1/2-inch-thick) slices Italian bread, lightly toasted**
  1/2 **cup grated Asiago cheese**

1. Bring the water to a boil in a large covered pot over high heat. Add the cannellini, garlic, onion, parsley, bay leaf, and red pepper flakes. Lower the heat to medium, cover, and cook, stirring occasionally, for 1 hour.

2. Add the oil, carrots, celery, cauliflower, cabbage, tomato, oregano, fennel seeds, salt, and pepper. Cover and cook at a medium boil, stirring occasionally, for about 1 hour, or until the beans are just tender.

3. Preheat the oven to 400 degrees. Add the escarole to the soup and continue cooking, uncovered, at a medium boil, stirring occasionally, for about 25 minutes, or until the beans are very tender and the escarole is tender. Taste for seasonings.

4. Spray a large baking pan with nonstick cooking spray. Arrange the toasted bread evenly in the baking pan. Ladle the soup into the pan, over the bread. Sprinkle the cheese evenly over the soup. Bake for 30 minutes, or until the soup is bubbling and the cheese is melted.

Zuppa Pavese

SERVES 6

I first enjoyed this soup during a recent visit to Naples and have been making it at home ever since. You first need to prepare a flavorful broth, which you will use to poach an egg for each serving. Place a slice of toasted Italian bread in individual bowls and ladle the soup and a poached egg over the toast.

3   tablespoons extra virgin olive oil
1   tablespoon butter or soybean margarine
1   large shallot, finely chopped
1   large leek, white and pale green parts only, well washed and finely chopped
1   large clove garlic, finely chopped
1   large yellow onion, finely chopped
1   large parsnip, peeled and finely chopped
3   medium carrots, peeled and finely chopped
3   ribs celery, finely chopped
1/4 cup finely chopped flat-leaf parsley
1   large bay leaf
    Salt and pepper to taste
1   (35-ounce) can Italian whole peeled tomatoes in juice, squeezed with your hands to crush
2   quarts water
1   teaspoon dried sage
5   fresh basil leaves
1/4 cup A-1 Bold & Spicy steak sauce
6   eggs
6   (1-inch-thick) slices Italian bread, lightly toasted

1. Heat the oil and butter in a large pot over medium heat. Add the shallot, leek, garlic, onion, parsnip, carrots, celery, parsley, bay leaf, salt, and pepper. Stir well to coat the vegetables with the oil. Cover and cook, stirring occasionally, for 15 minutes, or until the vegetables have softened.

2. Add the tomatoes, water, sage, basil, and steak sauce. Cover, raise the heat to high, and bring to a boil. Lower the heat to medium-low and cook at a medium boil, stirring occasionally, for about 45 minutes, or until the soup has reduced a little. Taste for seasonings.

3. Carefully crack open one egg at a time and drop it into the broth, allowing each egg to set for about 20 seconds before adding the next one. Cook for 5 minutes.

4. To serve the soup, place the slices of toasted bread in individual bowls, then ladle the soup and 1 cooked egg into each bowl.

Tomato and Cabbage Soup

SERVES 8

This soup is light and flavorful, perfect for any time of the year. Serve it with Italian bread for dunking and Salad from Sorrento (page 92) for a delicious lunch or light supper.

 3 tablespoons extra virgin olive oil
 1 tablespoon butter or soybean margarine
 1 large leek, white and pale green parts only, washed well and finely chopped
 2 large cloves garlic, finely chopped
 1 large head green cabbage, coarsely chopped
 1/2 head cauliflower, coarsely chopped
 1/4 cup finely chopped flat-leaf parsley
   Salt and pepper to taste
 1 (28-ounce) can Italian whole peeled tomatoes in juice, squeezed with your hands to crush
 2 quarts water
 1 large bay leaf
 2 teaspoons dried sage

1. Heat the oil and butter in a stockpot over medium heat. Add the leek, garlic, cabbage, cauliflower, parsley, salt, and pepper. Cover and cook, stirring occasionally, for 20 minutes, or until the vegetables have softened and released some of their moisture.

2. Add the tomatoes, water, bay leaf, and sage. Cover, raise the heat to high, and bring to a boil. Lower the heat to medium and cook at a medium boil, stirring occasionally, for one hour, or until the soup is reduced by about a third. Taste for seasonings.

Lentil Soup

SERVES 8

Lentil soup is loaded with vitamins and minerals. You can use a variety of vegetables, depending on what's available, but celery is one of my favorites for this hearty soup.

4 quarts water
1 pound lentils, picked over
1 bay leaf
5 tablespoons extra virgin olive oil
4 large cloves garlic, finely chopped
1 medium yellow onion, finely chopped
8 ribs celery, cut into 1/2-inch-thick slices, including leaves
6 medium carrots, peeled and cut into 1/2-inch-thick slices
1 large bulb fennel, cut into bite-size pieces
1 (6-ounce) can tomato paste
1/4 cup finely chopped flat-leaf parsley
Salt and pepper to taste
1 (10-ounce) bag spinach, well washed and coarsely chopped
2 cups tubetti pasta, cooked according to package directions

1. Place the water, lentils, and bay leaf in a large pot. Cover and bring to a boil over high heat. Lower the heat to medium.

2. Add the oil, garlic, onion, celery, carrots, fennel, tomato paste, parsley, salt, and pepper. Stir well to mix. Cover and cook at a medium-high boil (the soup will return to a boil after about 5 minutes), stirring occasionally, for about 1 hour, or until the lentils and celery are tender.

3. Add the spinach. Stir well to mix. Cover and continue cooking, stirring occasionally, for 5 minutes, or until the spinach is tender. Stir in the cooked pasta. Taste for seasonings.

Fresh Tomato Soup with Garlic Toasts

Serves 8

At the end of summer, when home gardens and farms are overflowing with fragrant ripe tomatoes, my thoughts always turn to this soup. I prepare it with plum, cherry, and beefsteak tomatoes, but any combination is fine, just as long as they are ripe and fresh. While vine-ripened tomatoes are now available year-round, the cost tends to be astounding, so you might want to save this recipe for summer.

> 2 tablespoons extra virgin olive oil
> 1 large sweet onion (Vidalia is best), finely chopped
> 1 large clove garlic, finely chopped
> 5 pounds ripe tomatoes, coarsely chopped, including the juices
> 1/4 cup coarsely chopped flat-leaf parsley
> 1 1/2 tablespoons chopped fresh oregano
> 1 tablespoon fresh rosemary leaves
>   Salt and pepper to taste
> 2 quarts water
> 1/4 cup Arborio rice (Italian risotto rice)

Garlic Toasts:
> 2 tablespoons extra virgin olive oil
> 3 large cloves garlic, finely minced
> 8 (1/2-inch-thick) slices Italian bread
>   Salt and pepper to taste

1. Heat the oil in a large pot over medium-low heat. Add the onion, garlic, tomatoes, parsley, oregano, and rosemary. Sprinkle with salt and pepper. Stir to mix. Cover and cook, stirring occasionally, for 15 minutes, or until the tomatoes are soft and have released their juices.

2. Add the water. Raise the heat to high, cover, and bring to a boil. Remove the cover and lower the heat to medium. Cook, uncovered, at a medium boil, stirring occasionally, for 1 hour, or until the soup is reduced slightly. Stir in the rice. Continue cooking at a medium boil, stirring frequently, for another hour, or until the rice is soft.

3. Meanwhile, prepare the garlic toasts. Preheat the oven to 350 degrees. Measure the oil into a small bowl. Add the garlic and whisk to combine. Arrange the slices of bread, cut side down, in a single layer on a nonstick cookie sheet. Bake the bread for 10 minutes, or until just firm to the touch. Turn the slices over and bake the other side for 10 minutes.

4. Remove from the oven and, using a pastry brush, brush the top of the toasts with the oil and garlic mixture. Spoon any remaining garlic evenly on the toasts.

5. Set the garlic toasts in individual bowls and ladle the soup over them. Serve with freshly ground black pepper.

Pasta e Fagioli

SERVES 8

Every Italian family has its own favorite recipe for pasta e fagioli, *or "macaroni and beans," as my mom called it. This delicious dish is pureed smooth after it's cooked, and it tastes best with a slice of bread spread with a thin layer of peanut butter. This may sound unusual, but trust me, it is truly wonderful.*

  4 **quarts water**
  1 **pound dried great northern beans, picked over**
  3 **tablespoons extra virgin olive oil**
  4 **large cloves garlic, coarsely chopped**
 1/2 **cup finely chopped fresh sage**
  1 **teaspoon dried sage**
     Salt and pepper to taste
  1 **(6-ounce) can tomato paste**
  8 **ounces ziti, cooked according to package directions**

1. Measure the water and beans into a stockpot. Cover and bring to a boil over high heat. Lower the heat to medium-low and cook, covered, at a medium boil for 1 hour, stirring occasionally.

2. Add the oil, garlic, sage, salt, pepper, and tomato paste. Stir well to combine. Cover and continue cooking at a medium boil, stirring occasionally, for another 1 1/2 hours, or until the beans are soft. Taste for seasonings.

3. If you have a hand blender, use it to puree the soup until smooth. Or puree the soup in a food processor, being careful not to burn yourself.

4. Return the pureed soup to the pot and reheat over low heat if desired. To serve, ladle the soup into soup bowls and top each serving with one-eighth of the cooked ziti, using a spoon to push the ziti down into the soup. Sprinkle with freshly ground black pepper.

Lentil and Sausage Soup

SERVES 8

Although we consume a variety of beans in our house, lentils remain the most popular. I cook them with any number of vegetables and often add pasta, barley, or rice. Lentils with sausage is one of the many scrumptious ways my grandmother prepared this fiber-rich, protein- and iron-packed bean. This healthful, spicy soup has a stewlike consistency.

12 ounces lentils, picked over
3 quarts water
3 tablespoons extra virgin olive oil
2 tablespoons tomato paste
2 bay leaves
5 large cloves garlic, cut into thick slices
1 cup coarsely chopped flat-leaf parsley
1 large sweet onion, finely chopped
1 large bunch celery, cut into 1-inch-thick slices (about 12 ribs)
1 tablespoon fennel seeds
Salt and pepper to taste
$1/2$ teaspoon red pepper flakes
$1/8$ teaspoon ground red pepper
$1/2$ cup Arborio rice (Italian risotto rice)
1 pound meatless sausage links, preferably Italian style, cut into 1-inch lengths

1. Place all the ingredients except the sausages in a heavy stockpot. Stir well to mix. Cover and bring to a boil over high heat. Lower the heat to medium-low and cook at a medium-low boil, stirring frequently, for about 1 hour, or until the celery is tender and the soup is thickened.

2. Stir in the sausages. Cover and continue cooking at a medium-low boil for 15 minutes, stirring occasionally. Taste for seasonings.

Vegetable Soup with Chicory and Escarole

Serves 8

This soup is made with the freshest vegetables the season has to offer. During the fall and winter months I often add one of my favorite vegetables—cardoon (my grandmother called it cardone). *Cardoon resembles a large bunch of celery and tastes like the stem of artichokes. Its flavor enhances a vegetable soup, and I encourage you to seek it out.*

3　tablespoons butter, soybean margarine, or extra virgin olive oil
1　large sweet onion, finely chopped
2　large cloves garlic, coarsely chopped
　　Salt and pepper to taste
2　large parsnips, peeled, cut in half lengthwise, then cut into $1/2$-inch pieces
3　large ribs celery, finely chopped
1　ripe large tomato, chopped, including juices
1　bunch cardoon (about 1 pound), ribs peeled, finely chopped
3　quarts water
1　cup coarsely chopped flat-leaf parsley
2　tablespoons coarsely chopped fresh basil
2　bay leaves
1　large head chicory (about 1 pound), cut into 1-inch pieces
1　large head escarole (about 1 pound), cut into 1-inch pieces
3　medium zucchini, cut into $1/2$-inch pieces
3　medium baking potatoes, peeled and diced
$2/3$　cup pastina (tiny pasta bits) or acini de pepe pasta

1. Heat the butter in a stockpot over medium-low heat. Add the onion, garlic, salt, and pepper. Cook, stirring occasionally, for 5 minutes, or until the onion is softened but not browned.

2. Add the parsnips, celery, tomato, cardoon, water, parsley, basil, and bay leaves. Raise the heat to high, cover, and bring to a boil. Lower the heat to medium-low and cook, covered, at a medium-low boil for 10 minutes, stirring occasionally.

3. Add the chicory and escarole. Stir well to mix. Cover and continue cooking, stirring occasionally, for another 30 minutes, or until the celery and cardoon are crisp-tender.

4. Add the zucchini and potatoes. Cover and continue cooking, stirring frequently, for about 15 minutes, or until the potatoes are tender.

5. Add the pastina. Cover and continue cooking, stirring frequently, for 8 to 10 minutes, or until the pastina is tender. Taste for seasonings.

Split Pea Soup with Meatless Hot Dogs

SERVES 8

On the rare occasion when my mom prepared a ham, she would always use the ham bone to flavor a split pea soup. I hate to admit it, but I loved that soup! Of course, as my (and my mom's) diet changed, ham was no longer eaten, but this soup brings back all the distinct flavor without any of the guilt. Most meatless hot dogs (and many are now available from supermarkets or health foods stores) are low in fat or fat-free. They have a rich, smoky flavor and a meaty texture and work wonderfully in this soup. I use Yves brand fat-free Jumbo Veggie Dogs in this recipe.

$1/4$ cup extra virgin olive oil

1 large sweet onion, coarsely chopped

3 large cloves garlic, coarsely chopped

6 medium carrots, peeled and cut into bite-size pieces

6 ribs celery, cut into bite-size pieces, including leaves

$1/2$ cup coarsely chopped flat-leaf parsley

10 leaves fresh basil
   Salt and pepper to taste

3 quarts water

1 (14- or 16-ounce) package green split peas, picked over

2 bay leaves

1 head escarole (about $1^1/4$ pounds), cut into 2-inch pieces

1 (14- or 16-ounce) package meatless hot dogs, cut into $1/2$-inch pieces

1. Heat the oil in a large pot over medium-low heat. Add the onion, garlic, carrots, celery, parsley, basil, salt, and pepper. Cover and cook for 15 minutes, stirring occasionally until the vegetables have softened and released some of their moisture.

2. Add the water. Cover, raise the heat to high, and bring to a boil. Add the split peas, bay leaves, and escarole. Lower the heat to medium-low. Cover and cook, stirring occasionally, for $1^1/2$ hours, or until the peas and vegetables are soft.

3. Add the meatless hot dogs. Cover and continue cooking for 4 minutes, stirring occasionally. Taste for seasonings.

Minestrone

SERVES 8

In our house minestrone is always made with odd lots of vegetables—three or four carrots left in the bin, two or three remaining ribs of celery, a quarter head of cabbage— whatever vegetables we have on hand. Our minestrone is always delicious and interesting and contains an abundance of healthful, colorful vegetables.

 1/4 cup olive oil
 1 small yellow onion, finely chopped
 4 large cloves garlic, coarsely chopped
 1 medium leek, white and pale green parts only, well washed and cut into
   1/2-inch pieces
 3 medium carrots, peeled and chopped
 3 ribs celery, chopped
 3 quarts water
 1 (12-ounce) package navy pea beans, picked over
 1 (6-ounce) can tomato paste
 1/2 cup coarsely chopped flat-leaf parsley
10 large fresh basil leaves
 2 large bay leaves
 1 tablespoon chopped fresh oregano or 1/2 teaspoon dried
   Salt and pepper to taste
 3 medium baking potatoes, peeled and cut into 1/2-inch cubes
 2 small zucchini, cut into 1/2-inch pieces
 1/4 medium head green cabbage, coarsely chopped
12 green beans, trimmed and cut into 1-inch lengths
 1 small head escarole (about 12 ounces), coarsely chopped
 1/4 cup pastina (tiny pasta bits)

 1. Heat the oil in a large pot over medium-low heat. Add the onion, garlic, leek, carrots, and celery. Stir to coat the vegetables with the oil. Cover and cook, stirring occasionally, for 5 minutes, or until the vegetables have softened and released some of their moisture.

 2. Add the water and the navy pea beans. Cover, raise the heat to high, and bring to a boil. Lower the heat to medium-low, cover, and cook at a medium boil for 30 minutes, stirring occasionally.

3. Add the tomato paste, parsley, basil, bay leaves, oregano, salt, and pepper. Cover and continue cooking, stirring occasionally, for 30 minutes, or until the beans are barely tender.

4. Add the potatoes, zucchini, cabbage, green beans, and escarole. Stir well to mix. Cover and continue cooking, stirring occasionally, for about 50 minutes, or until the beans are tender.

5. Stir in the pastina. Cover and continue cooking, stirring occasionally, for 6 to 10 minutes, or until the pastina is soft. Taste for seasonings.

Chickpea and Tomato Soup with Pasta Shells

SERVES 8

In my family chickpeas, also known as garbanzo beans, are the most versatile food. These protein-packed beans are delicious in stews, salads, spreads, dips, sauces, and of course soups like minestrone and this spicy, richly flavored, stewlike soup. Serve it with crusty bread for sopping up all the juices and a simple tossed salad for a terrific supper.

3 tablespoons extra virgin olive oil
2 medium yellow onions, finely chopped
6 large cloves garlic, coarsely chopped
2 quarts water
1 pound dried chickpeas (garbanzo beans), picked over
2 (28-ounce) cans Italian whole peeled tomatoes in juice, squeezed with your hands to crush
1/2 cup coarsely chopped flat-leaf parsley
1/4 teaspoon red pepper flakes
1 tablespoon fresh rosemary leaves or 1 teaspoon dried
1 teaspoon dried oregano
2 bay leaves
1/4 cup dry red wine
Salt and pepper to taste
1 large bunch Swiss chard (about 1 pound), bottom 6 inches of stem trimmed off, remaining stems and leaves cut into 1-inch pieces
1 pound medium pasta shells, cooked according to package directions
Freshly grated pecorino Romano cheese (optional)

1. Heat the oil in a large pot over medium-low heat. Add the onions and garlic. Cover and cook, stirring occasionally, for 5 minutes, or until the onions and garlic are softened but not burned.

2. Add the water and chickpeas. Cover, raise the heat to high, and bring to a boil. Lower the heat to medium-low and continue cooking, stirring occasionally, for 1 hour.

3. Add the tomatoes, parsley, red pepper flakes, rosemary, oregano, bay leaves, wine, salt, and pepper. Cover and continue cooking, stirring occasionally, for $1^1/_2$ hours, or until the chickpeas are just tender.

4. Add the Swiss chard. Stir well to mix. Cover and continue cooking, stirring occasionally, for about 30 minutes, or until the Swiss chard is tender. Stir in the cooked pasta shells. Taste for seasonings. Serve with freshly grated pecorino Romano, if desired.

Fennel Salad

SERVES 4

Fresh fennel has a refreshing mild licorice flavor. In our family we eat it raw in salads or on an antipasto platter, just drizzled with a little olive oil and fresh lemon juice. Occasionally we sauté or roast fennel, which also is delicious. (See Sautéed Fennel, page 51.)

1   large bulb fennel, bottom $1/4$ inch trimmed off
2   ribs celery, cut into $1/4$-inch-thick slices
2   tablespoons extra virgin olive oil
2   tablespoons fresh lemon juice (about $1/2$ lemon)
     Salt and pepper to taste
1   tablespoon finely chopped flat-leaf parsley
12 oil-cured black olives, pitted

Cut the fennel into thin slices lengthwise. Arrange on a platter. Scatter the celery over the fennel. Drizzle the olive oil and lemon juice evenly over the top. Sprinkle with salt and pepper. Scatter the parsley and olives over the top.

Italian Potato Salad

SERVES 6

During our most recent trip to Italy, we found this colorful potato salad in most of the cities and towns we visited. It is a fine addition to your summer picnic or to a meal at any time of the year. Try it with Italian Hamburgers (page 191) and Salad from Sorrento (page 92).

6 medium baking potatoes
2 medium carrots, peeled and diced
1 cup frozen green peas, thawed
1 small yellow onion, finely chopped
2 tablespoons finely chopped flat-leaf parsley
1/4 cup mayonnaise or soy mayonnaise
1/4 cup low-fat sour cream
2 tablespoons milk or soy milk
Salt and pepper to taste

1. Cook the potatoes in a large pot of lightly salted boiling water for about 20 minutes, then add the carrots and continue cooking for 3 to 4 minutes, or until the potatoes are fork-tender. Drain.

2. When the potatoes are cool enough to handle, peel them and cut in half lengthwise. Cut the halves into thirds and place in a large bowl.

3. Add the remaining ingredients and toss well to combine. Taste for seasonings. Serve immediately or chilled.

Salad from Sorrento

SERVES 6

Sorrento is famous for its beautiful handmade linens. During our recent trip to Italy, we visited the city and ate one memorable meal after another. This salad was one of those meals. It makes a fine lunch when served with good bread.

8 ounces mixed baby greens (mesclun)
1 small yellow onion, cut into thin slices and separated into rings
1 large bunch arugula (about 4 ounces), well washed
1 small clove garlic, minced
4 radishes, thinly sliced
1 medium carrot, peeled and thinly sliced
1 small bulb fennel, cut into thin slices
1 (15-ounce) can chickpeas, drained
3 tablespoons extra virgin olive oil
2 tablespoons fresh lemon juice (about $1/2$ lemon)
1 tablespoon finely chopped flat-leaf parsley
Salt and pepper to taste

Place the ingredients in a salad bowl in the order in which they are listed. Toss to mix evenly. Taste for seasonings.

Mushroom Salad with Celery and Parmigiano Curls

SERVES 4

My grandmother often made a delightful little salad of celery and onions tossed with olive oil and fresh lemon juice and topped with slices of Parmigiano-Reggiano cheese. When I was in Italy, many of the restaurants offered a similar combination that also included sliced mushrooms.

Note: Try to buy Parmigiano-Reggiano cheese rather than an ordinary Parmesan cheese because the flavor and texture are superior.

- 8 ounces cremini mushrooms, thinly sliced
- 3 ribs celery, cut into thin slices, including leaves
- 1 small sweet onion, cut into thin slices and separated into rings
- 3 tablespoons extra virgin olive oil
- 3 tablespoons fresh lemon juice (about 1 lemon)
  Salt and pepper to taste
- 2 ounces Parmigiano-Reggiano cheese

Place the mushrooms, celery, and onion in a bowl. Toss gently to mix. Drizzle the oil and lemon juice evenly over the salad and toss again. Sprinkle with salt and pepper. Toss gently to mix. Taste for seasonings. Turn the salad out onto a serving plate. Using a potato peeler, scrape the cheese to make curls. Scatter evenly over the salad.

Broccoli and Potato Salad with Green Sauce

SERVES 6 TO 8

This salad was inspired by the beautiful pesto sauces on the menus of many restaurants in Genoa. My variation is made with flat-leaf parsley, capers, lemon juice, extra virgin olive oil, and bread soaked in soy milk, which gives this sauce an appealing texture.

3 **(1-inch-thick) slices Italian or French bread**
1 **cup soy milk**
4 **medium baking potatoes, peeled and cut into 1-inch cubes**
   Salt and pepper to taste
1 **large bunch broccoli (about 12 ounces), bottom 1 inch trimmed off**
1 **cup coarsely chopped flat-leaf parsley**
4 **large cloves garlic, coarsely chopped**
2 **tablespoons capers, drained**
3 **tablespoons fresh lemon juice (about 1 lemon)**
1/4 **cup extra virgin olive oil**

1. Cut each slice of bread into quarters. Place in a bowl and pour 1/2 cup of the soy milk evenly over the bread. Set aside to allow the bread to absorb the soy milk.

2. Meanwhile, place the potatoes in a large pot and add water to cover by 3 inches. Sprinkle with salt. Cover and bring to a boil over high heat.

3. Cut the broccoli stems into 1/2-inch diagonal slices. Place in a bowl and set aside. Separate the florets and place in another bowl. Set aside.

4. Once the water begins to boil, lower the heat to medium and cook the potatoes, covered, at a medium boil for 7 minutes. Add the sliced broccoli stems, cover, and continue cooking for 2 minutes. Add the florets, cover, and continue cooking for 3 minutes. Drain the potatoes and broccoli in a colander. Turn into a large bowl. Set aside while you make the green sauce.

5. Place the soaked bread and any soy milk remaining in the bowl in a blender. Add the parsley, garlic, capers, lemon juice, salt, pepper, oil, and remaining 1/2 cup soy milk. Carefully mix the ingredients with a rubber spatula. Cover the blender and pulse the mixture 3 or 4 times, stopping to mix the ingredients. Blend on high speed for 20 to 30 seconds, or until well blended, stopping occasionally to scrape down the sides. Taste for seasonings.

6. Pour the sauce over the broccoli and potatoes, using a rubber spatula to scrape the blender clean. Gently toss the salad until it is coated with the sauce. Taste for seasonings. Serve immediately or chilled.

White Bean and Mint Salad

SERVES 6

I've used mint in many dishes over the years, from fish to zucchini, and this fiber-rich salad is one of the easiest to make.

1 pound dried great northern beans or cannellini, picked over
3 quarts water
3 large cloves garlic, finely chopped
4 vine-ripened tomatoes, cut into cubes, including juices
1 small sweet onion, finely chopped
2 tablespoons extra virgin olive oil
3 tablespoons coarsely chopped fresh mint or 1 teaspoon dried
Salt and pepper to taste

1. Place the beans and water in a large pot. Cover and bring to a boil over high heat. Lower the heat to medium and cook, covered, for about $1^1/_2$ hours, or until tender. Drain the beans in a colander, then turn them into a bowl.

2. Add the garlic, tomatoes, and onion and toss to mix. Drizzle the oil evenly on top toss gently to combine. Scatter the mint leaves over the salad, add salt and pepper, and toss gently but thoroughly. Taste for seasonings. Serve immediately or refrigerate and serve chilled.

Red Oak Lettuce, Pears, Walnuts, and Gorgonzola in Lime Vinaigrette

Serves 6

This is the perfect salad to enjoy during the fall, when pears are at their juicy best. A bit of Gorgonzola cheese adds a pungent flavor that pairs nicely with the sweetness of the pears.

2 ripe large Bartlett pears, cored and cut into $^1/_2$-inch cubes
$^1/_4$ cup chopped walnuts
1 head red oak lettuce (about 12 ounces) or your favorite lettuce, torn into 2-inch pieces
1 large clove garlic, finely chopped
3 tablespoons extra virgin olive oil
5 tablespoons fresh lime juice (about 2 limes)
1 tablespoon cider vinegar
  Salt and pepper to taste
6 ounces Gorgonzola cheese (preferably imported from Italy)

1. Heat a large nonstick skillet over medium heat. Spray with olive oil cooking spray. Add the pears and walnuts and cook, stirring occasionally, for 4 minutes, or until the pears are softened and the walnuts are toasted. Remove from the heat.

2. Place the torn lettuce in a large salad bowl. Scatter the garlic over the lettuce. In a small bowl, whisk the oil, lime juice, vinegar, salt, and pepper. Taste for seasonings.

3. Add the pears and walnuts to the lettuce. Toss to mix. Pour the dressing evenly over the salad and toss to coat the leaves. Scatter the Gorgonzola cheese evenly over the salad. Toss to mix. Serve immediately.

Sausage Salad with Arugula and Tomatoes

SERVES 4

This is a richly flavored whole-meal salad of browned sausages in balsamic vinegar with tomatoes, cremini mushrooms, and arugula. This flavorful concoction is topped with grated ricotta salata, a semifirm sheep's milk cheese from Italy.

8 links meatless sausages (preferably Italian style), cut into 1-inch lengths
2 tablespoons balsamic vinegar
1 large bunch arugula (about 4 ounces)
2 ripe medium tomatoes, cut into 1/4-inch-thick wedges
3 medium cremini mushrooms, cut into thin slices
2 tablespoons extra virgin olive oil
   Salt and pepper to taste
2 ounces ricotta salata cheese, coarsely grated

1. Spray a large nonstick skillet with olive oil cooking spray. Heat over medium heat. Arrange the sausage in a single layer in the skillet. Cook for about 2 minutes on each side, or until medium brown, using tongs to turn. Drizzle 1 tablespoon of the vinegar evenly over the sausage.

2. Place the arugula, tomatoes, and mushrooms in a large bowl. Drizzle the oil evenly over the salad. Toss to coat. Drizzle the remaining tablespoon of vinegar evenly over the salad. Sprinkle with salt and pepper. Toss to mix and coat the ingredients.

3. Arrange the salad on a platter. Scatter the sausage over the salad. Scatter the grated ricotta salata evenly over the salad. Serve immediately.

Panzanella
(Bread and Vegetable Salad)

SERVES 6

Every Italian family I know has its own recipe for panzanella, *the inescapable (luckily!) summer salad that is made with summer tomatoes and Italian bread—and whatever else you may want to add.*

  7 (1-inch-thick) slices Italian bread, cut into 1-inch cubes (about 9 cups)
  5 ripe medium tomatoes, cut into 1-inch-thick wedges, including juices
  1 medium cucumber, seeded and diced
10 large fresh basil leaves
  2 tablespoons coarsely chopped fresh oregano
  1 large sweet onion, cut into 1/4-inch-thick ribs
  3 tablespoons extra virgin olive oil
  1 tablespoon red wine vinegar
    Salt and pepper to taste

1. Place the bread cubes in a large mixing bowl. Add the tomatoes and their juices. Toss well to coat the bread with the tomato juices.

2. Add the cucumber, basil, oregano, and onion. Toss to mix. Drizzle the oil evenly over the mixture. Toss well to coat. Drizzle the vinegar over the salad. Add salt and pepper to taste. Toss well to mix. Taste for seasonings.

Broccoli Salad

SERVES 6

A simple combination of broccoli, garlic, and lemon can yield dishes of unbelievable range and flavor.

Note: My editor, Julia Serebrinsky, adds roasted slivered almonds to this salad and now I do too.

> **1 large bunch broccoli (about 12 ounces)**
> **3 tablespoons extra virgin olive oil**
> **6 large cloves garlic, cut into thick slices**
>   **Salt and pepper to taste**
> **3 tablespoons fresh lemon juice (about 1 lemon)**

1. Bring 2 quarts of lightly salted water to a boil in a large pot over high heat. Meanwhile, cut off and discard the bottom 1 inch of the broccoli stems. Peel the stems of the broccoli to remove the tough skin. Separate the stems from the florets. Cut the stems into 1/2-inch diagonal slices. Break the florets into medium-size pieces.

2. When the water comes to a boil, drop in the stems of the broccoli. Cook for 2 minutes, then add the florets and continue cooking for 3 minutes. Drain. Turn into a bowl.

3. Heat the oil in a skillet over medium heat. Add the garlic, salt, and pepper. Cook, turning occasionally, for 3 minutes, or until the garlic is golden brown but not burned.

4. Pour the garlic and oil over the broccoli, using a rubber spatula to scrape out the skillet. Stir to mix. Add the lemon juice and stir to mix. Taste for seasonings. Serve immediately or chilled.

Green Bean and Tomato Salad

SERVES 6

Now that flavorful vine-ripened tomatoes are available year-round, we make this delicious salad even in January.

12 ounces green beans, trimmed, cut in half
 6 ripe plum tomatoes, cut into quarters
 1 small yellow onion, cut into thin slices and separated into rings
 1 large clove garlic, finely chopped
 3 tablespoons extra virgin olive oil
 6 large fresh basil leaves, cut in half
    Salt and pepper to taste

Cook the green beans in lightly salted boiling water for about 5 minutes, or until just tender. Drain. Turn into a bowl. Add the remaining ingredients. Toss well to combine. Taste for seasonings. Serve at room temperature or chilled.

Salad from Capri

SERVES 4

This is a beautiful salad of fresh mozzarella, sliced tomatoes, and fresh basil drizzled with extra virgin olive oil. I've served it with crusty Italian bread and fresh lemonade for a light lunch on the patio during the summer, and it has always been a great hit.

Note: Use the fresh mozzarella that is sold floating in a pool of milk in the deli section of many supermarkets.

12 **ounces fresh mozzarella, drained and cut into $1/4$-inch-thick slices**
 1 **large or 2 medium tomatoes, cut into $1/4$-inch-thick slices**
12 **fresh basil leaves**
 3 **tablespoons extra virgin olive oil**
    Salt and pepper to taste

On a platter, arrange alternating slices of mozzarella and slices of tomato, overlapping them slightly. Insert the basil leaves between the tomatoes and mozzarella. Drizzle the olive oil evenly over the salad. Sprinkle with salt and pepper.

Bacon, Arugula, and Tomato on Italian Bread with Basil Mayonnaise

SERVES 4

Here's a healthful Italian version of the BLT. For dairy-free mayonnaise I use Nay-onnaise brand, found in health foods stores.

- 1/4 **cup fat-free dairy-free mayonnaise**
- 10 **large leaves fresh basil, finely chopped**
- 8 **strips meatless bacon**
- 1 **bunch arugula (about 4 ounces), trimmed of tough stems**
- 1 **ripe large tomato, cut into 1/4-inch-thick slices**
- 1 **tablespoon extra virgin olive oil**
- 1 **tablespoon balsamic vinegar**
  Salt and pepper to taste
- 1 **loaf Italian bread, cut into 3-inch-wide sandwich pieces**

1. Combine the mayonnaise and basil in a cup. Stir to mix well.

2. Heat a large nonstick skillet over medium-high heat. Spray the skillet with olive oil cooking spray. Arrange the bacon strips in a single layer in the hot skillet. Cook for 2 to 3 minutes, or until medium brown. Turn and cook the other side for 2 to 3 minutes, or until medium brown.

3. Place the arugula and sliced tomatoes in a bowl. Drizzle the oil and vinegar evenly over them and sprinkle with salt and pepper. Toss well to coat evenly. Taste for seasonings.

4. Cut each sandwich piece in half, horizontally. Cut each of the browned bacon strips in half. To assemble the sandwiches, spread the bottom half of each sandwich piece with 1 tablespoon of the basil mayonnaise, then top with 4 half strips of bacon and one-fourth of the arugula and tomato mixture. Cover the sandwich with the top half of the bread.

Salad of Oranges, Red Onions, and Oil~Cured Black Olives

SERVES 6

Serve this colorful salad with Potato and Onion Frittata (page 159) for a light dinner.

  1 small head romaine lettuce, torn into 2-inch pieces
  4 large oranges, peeled and cut into $1/4$-inch-thick slices
  1 medium red onion, cut into thin slices and separated into rings
 24 oil-cured black olives
  2 tablespoons extra virgin olive oil
  1 tablespoon balsamic vinegar
  2 tablespoons coarsely chopped flat-leaf parsley
     Salt and pepper to taste

Arrange the lettuce on a large serving platter. Arrange the orange slices on top of the lettuce in a circular pattern, overlapping them slightly. Scatter the onion rings and black olives over the salad. Drizzle the oil and vinegar evenly over the salad. Scatter the parsley over the salad. Sprinkle lightly with salt and pepper.

"Beef" Salad

Serves 4

Both my grandmother and my mom often prepared a main-dish salad using the beef from the shank after making their beef, vegetable, and noodle soup. They would cut the beef into pieces and combine it with onion, olive oil, and red wine vinegar. Although this combination is delicious as a salad, I liked it best in a sandwich on Italian bread, with lettuce leaves and a thin layer of mayonnaise on the bread. Luckily, seitan, also known as wheat meat, is a delicious and healthful replacement for the beef that my mom and I no longer eat. I only wish my grandmother could taste this flavorful version of her salad. She would surely approve.

Note: I use White Wave brand seitan for this recipe, but there are several brands in health foods markets. Buy several packs and freeze them for future use.

- 1 **quart water**
- 1 **bay leaf**
- 1 **ripe medium tomato, coarsely chopped, including juices**
- 1 **small yellow onion, coarsely chopped**
- 1 **teaspoon dried oregano**
  Salt and pepper to taste
- 2 **(8-ounce) packages seitan, including juices**
- 1 **medium sweet onion, cut into 1/4-inch-thick ribs**
- 1/4 **cup coarsely chopped flat-leaf parsley**
- 3 **tablespoons extra virgin olive oil**
- 3 **tablespoons red wine vinegar**

1. Place the water, bay leaf, tomato, small onion, 1/4 teaspoon of the oregano, the salt, and pepper in a large pot. Cover and bring to a boil over high heat. Lower the heat to medium and cook, covered, for 20 minutes, stirring occasionally. Taste for seasonings.

2. Add the seitan and the juices from the package to the pot. Cover and continue cooking for 10 minutes, stirring occasionally. Using tongs, remove the seitan pieces to a colander. Reserve the broth for another use (perhaps in a soup). Cut the seitan into 1-inch pieces and place in a bowl.

3. Add the onion ribs, parsley, oil, vinegar, remaining 3/4 teaspoon oregano, and salt and pepper. Toss well. Taste for seasonings. Serve at room temperature or chilled.

Sun~Dried Tomato Vinaigrette

MAKES ABOUT 1¹/₃ CUPS

Prepare three or four dressings and store them in bottles in your refrigerator for up to two weeks. This will give you both variety and convenience.

- **1 cup olive oil**
- **6 sun-dried tomatoes in oil, drained and coarsely chopped**
- **3 tablespoons fresh lemon juice (about 1 lemon)**
- **¹/₄ cup coarsely chopped flat-leaf parsley**
- **10 fresh basil leaves, coarsely chopped**
- **Salt and pepper to taste**

Place all the ingredients in a blender and whirl on high speed for about 20 seconds, or until well blended. Taste for seasonings. Turn into a jar, using a rubber spatula to scrape out the container, and refrigerate until needed.

Italian Dressing

MAKES 3 CUPS

This dressing—a chunky combination of peppers, onions, and tomato with olive oil, lemon juice, and red wine vinegar—was inspired by the man who runs Aniello's, a superb little Italian restaurant in my hometown. Its flavors are delightful, and its texture is a nice change from smooth dressings. Try it on a potato salad too.

1 **cup olive oil**
$1/4$ **cup red wine vinegar**
2 **tablespoons fresh lemon juice (about $1/2$ lemon)**
1 **green bell pepper, seeded and coarsely chopped**
1 **small yellow onion, coarsely chopped**
1 **medium tomato, coarsely chopped, including juices**
$1/4$ **cup coarsely chopped flat-leaf parsley**
1 **teaspoon dried oregano**
Salt and pepper to taste

Place all the ingredients in a blender and whirl on high speed for about 10 seconds, stopping once or twice to scrape down the sides of the container with a rubber spatula. Taste for seasonings. Turn into a jar. Refrigerate until needed.

Lemon~Mint Vinaigrette

MAKES 1½ CUPS

This lemon and herb dressing is perfect on any salad, vegetable, or pasta. It is also a delicious marinade for grilled portobello mushrooms.

- 1 **cup olive oil**
- 2 **large cloves garlic, coarsely chopped**
- ¼ **cup fresh lemon juice (about 1 lemon)**
- 10 **fresh basil leaves, coarsely chopped**
- 2 **tablespoons coarsely chopped fresh mint or 2 teaspoons dried**
- 1 **tablespoon capers, drained**
  Salt and pepper to taste

Place all the ingredients in a blender and whirl on high speed for about 10 seconds, stopping once or twice to scrape down the sides of the container with a rubber spatula. Taste for seasonings. Turn into a jar, using the spatula to scrape out the container. Refrigerate until needed.

Creamy Garlic Dressing

MAKES 2¹/₂ CUPS

This rich, garlicky dressing is excellent over a mixed salad or tossed with potatoes.

> 2 **cups sour cream**
> ¹/₄ **cup milk**
> 1 **tablespoon red wine vinegar**
> 5 **large cloves garlic, coarsely chopped**
>   **Salt and pepper to taste**

Place all the ingredients in a blender and whirl on high speed for 15 seconds, or until the mixture is smooth. Taste for seasonings. Turn into a wide jar, using a rubber spatula to scrape out the container. Refrigerate until needed.

Red Wine Vinaigrette

MAKES 1¼ CUPS

My Aunt Marge tosses her salads with this simple dressing that I have never tired of, not even after the thirty years she's been in the family.

1 **cup olive oil**
¼ **cup red wine vinegar**
1 **teaspoon dried oregano**
1 **teaspoon dried basil**
Salt and pepper to taste

Place all the ingredients in a blender and whirl on high speed for 10 seconds. Taste for seasonings. Turn into a jar with a tight-fitting lid. Refrigerate until needed.

Pesto Vinaigrette

Makes 1¹/₂ cups

Every summer at Claire's, we buy crates of fresh basil, then blend the leaves with olive oil to make fresh-tasting dressings and sauces. We toss the dressing over mixed green salads, potatoes, pastas, tortellini, and tomato salads. We even stir this dressing into mayonnaise to make a lovely green dip for vegetables and little toasts.

>   1 cup olive oil
>   4 large cloves garlic, coarsely chopped
>   1 cup fresh basil leaves, including stems
>   1 cup coarsely chopped flat-leaf parsley
>   2 tablespoons grated Parmigiano-Reggiano cheese
>   Salt and pepper to taste

Place the ingredients, in the order listed, in a blender and whirl on high speed for about 15 seconds, or until the mixture is well blended. Taste for seasonings. Turn into a jar. Refrigerate until needed.

Pastas and Sauces

Ziti with Asparagus, Onions, Eggs, and Parmesan
Potato Gnocchi
Tagliatelle Sorrentina
Macaroni with Peas
Pasta with Ricotta and Arugula
Semolina Gnocchi
Orecchiette with Kidney Bean Sauce
Penne with Sicilian Eggplant, Cherry Tomatoes, Leeks, and Peperoncini
Penne with Creamy Mushroom and Vodka Sauce
Penne with Creamy Tomato-Vegetable Sauce
Homemade Manicotti
Linguine with Pumpkin Sauce
Farfalle with Spinach, Tomatoes, and Wine
Pastina with Butter and Eggs
Spaghetti with Cauliflower, Parmigiano, and Eggs
Spinach and Ricotta Dumplings
Tagliatelle with Zucchini, Oyster Mushrooms, Lemon, and Mint
Eggplant Lasagne
Holiday Lasagne
Ricotta Gnocchi

Spaghetti with Olive Oil, Garlic Chips, and Capers
Holiday Marinara Sauce
Fresh Tomato Sauce
Basil-Scented Marinara Sauce

Ziti with Asparagus, Onions, Eggs, and Parmesan

SERVES 6

While the ziti tubes cook, you prepare a delicious sauce of onions and asparagus. Then you combine the cooked ziti with the vegetables and stir in eggs beaten with a little Parmigiano-Reggiano cheese. This dish makes a complete supper, and the leftovers taste terrific either chilled or reheated.

  1 **pound ziti**
$1/4$ **cup extra virgin olive oil**
  3 **medium sweet onions, cut into thick ribs**
  1 **large bunch asparagus (about 1 pound), bottom 2 inches trimmed off, stems cut into 1-inch diagonal slices**
    Salt and pepper to taste
  4 **eggs**
$1/2$ **cup freshly grated Parmigiano-Reggiano cheese**
$1/4$ **cup coarsely chopped flat-leaf parsley**
10 **large fresh basil leaves**

1. Bring a stockpot of lightly salted water to a boil over high heat and cook the ziti according to package directions. Before draining the pasta, reserve 1 cup of the cooking water.

2. Meanwhile, heat the oil in a large, deep skillet over medium heat. Add the onions, asparagus, salt, and pepper. Cook, stirring occasionally, for about 10 minutes, or until the onions are lightly browned and the asparagus are crisp-tender.

3. While the vegetables are cooking, combine the eggs, cheese, parsley, and basil in a bowl. Beat lightly with a whisk or fork and set aside.

4. Add the reserved pasta cooking water to the vegetables and stir to mix. Add the cooked ziti. Stir to mix thoroughly and to coat evenly.

5. Add the beaten eggs all at once and stir to coat the pasta evenly. Cook, stirring frequently, for 5 minutes, or until the eggs are set. Sprinkle additional pepper on top if desired.

Potato Gnocchi

SERVES 8+

A family friend, Teresa Vece, from the old neighborhood taught me how to make these gnocchi. Potato gnocchi (pronounced NYAW-kee*) are little dumplings, and although they can be found in the frozen foods section of most supermarkets, homemade ones are more delicious and flavorful. Making gnocchi can be an entire family effort. (In our family we make gnocchi along with a pot of marinara sauce). Serve with a tossed salad or Sautéed Spinach (page 54) for a typical Sunday meal.*

Note: Potato gnocchi are best when cooked the day they are made.

 6 **large baking potatoes, peeled and cut into quarters**
    Salt and pepper to taste
 4 **to 5 cups unbleached all-purpose flour**
 2 **eggs, lightly beaten**
 4 **cups Basil-Scented Marinara Sauce (page 150), heated**
 1/2 **cup grated Parmigiano-Reggiano cheese (optional)**

1. Bring a large, covered pot of lightly salted water to a boil over high heat. Add the potatoes. Cook for about 30 minutes until just fork tender. Drain into a colander. Add salt and pepper to taste.

2. Measure 2 cups of the flour into a large bowl. Using a ricer, rice the potatoes directly over the flour in the bowl. Using a large spoon, make a well in the middle of the riced potatoes and flour. Add the beaten eggs. Add 1 1/2 cups of the flour. Using a fork, work the mixture together to combine. Add additional flour, 1/4 cup at a time until the mixture holds together, but is not dry and crumbly. The amount of flour needed will depend on how much water is in the potatoes, and the humidity.

3. Dust a countertop or a large wooden cutting board with flour. Turn the potato gnocchi mixture onto the floured area. Knead lightly for about 10 minutes until the mixture is smooth, adding a little flour if the mixture becomes sticky.

4. Using your hands, roll the dough into a 22-inch loaf about the size of a long loaf of French bread. Cut off a 2-inch slice. Dust the board with a little flour. Roll this into a rope-shaped piece, about 21 inches long and 1 inch wide, using your fingers to roll it. Cut off $3/4$-inch nugget-sized pieces. Dust lightly with a little flour. Using your middle finger, gently push into the center of a nugget-sized piece, and gently roll the dough toward you, creating a deep depression in the center. Repeat with the remaining nuggets.

5. Transfer the gnocchi to a cookie sheet. Cut another 2-inch-thick slice from the remaining dough and repeat the process until you have rolled and shaped all of the dough.

6. Bring a large pot of lightly salted water to a boil over high heat. Add the gnocchi and cook, uncovered, gently stirring occasionally with a wooden spoon, for about 3 minutes, or until the gnocchi float to the surface and are tender to the bite. Drain the gnocchi and return them to the pot.

7. Ladle 1 cup of the heated marinara sauce over the gnocchi. Toss gently with wooden spoons to avoid breaking up the gnocchi. Turn into a serving bowl. Ladle additional sauce over the gnocchi. Sprinkle the cheese on top, if desired.

Tagliatelle Sorrentina

SERVES 6

Tagliatelle are wide noodles slightly narrower than fettuccine. In this dish they are tossed with a sauce made of crumbled hard Italian bread, capers, extra virgin olive oil, garlic, and onions. This is a quick-to-prepare rustic dish from Sorrento.

1 **pound tagliatelle**
6 **(1-inch-thick) slices of hard Italian bread**
5 **tablespoons extra virgin olive oil**
2 **large sweet onions, finely chopped**
4 **large cloves garlic, cut into thick slices**
   Salt and pepper to taste
3 **tablespoons capers, drained**
1 **teaspoon dried oregano**
1 **cup coarsely chopped flat-leaf parsley**

1. Bring a large pot of lightly salted water to a boil over high heat and cook the tagliatelle according to package directions. Before draining the pasta, reserve 1 cup of the cooking water. Meanwhile, crumble the bread into little pieces and set aside.

2. Heat the oil in a large pot over medium heat. Add the onions, garlic, salt, and pepper. Stir to coat onions with the oil. Cover and cook, stirring occasionally, for 10 minutes, or until the onions are softened.

3. Add the capers, oregano, parsley, and reserved pasta cooking water. Stir to mix. Cook for 5 minutes, stirring occasionally.

4. Add the cooked tagliatelle and the crumbled bread and remove the pot from the heat. Toss well to coat the pasta with the cooked onions. Serve immediately.

Macaroni with Peas

SERVES 6

In my grandmother's house pasta e piselli (*macaroni and peas*) *was prepared with pasta shells in a sauce of tomatoes and green peas. But her daughter-in-law, my Aunt Marge, prepared it differently, using a simple sauce of olive oil, onions, garlic, and canned green peas. I try to buy canned organic peas from a health foods store or super-market. The sauce is quick to prepare, making this dish a perfect weeknight supper. Just add a tossed salad and some Italian bread.*

1   **pound tubetti pasta (little pasta tubes)**
3   **tablespoons extra virgin olive oil**
2   **large sweet onions, coarsely chopped**
6   **large cloves garlic, coarsely chopped**
1   **teaspoon dried oregano**
2   **(14-ounce) cans green peas, including liquid**
1/4 **cup coarsely chopped flat-leaf parsley**
     Salt and pepper to taste

1. Bring a stockpot of lightly salted water to a boil over high heat and cook the pasta according to package directions. Before draining the pasta, reserve 2 cups of the cooking water.

2. Meanwhile, heat the oil in a large pot over medium-low heat. Add the onions and garlic, cover, and cook, stirring occasionally, for 10 minutes, or until the onions and garlic are golden brown but not burned.

3. Add the oregano, green peas and liquid, parsley, a little salt (canned peas are often salted), and pepper. Raise the heat to medium. Cover and cook at a medium boil, stirring occasionally, for 10 minutes.

4. Add the reserved pasta cooking water and cooked tubetti. Remove from the heat. Toss well to coat the pasta evenly. Taste for seasonings. Serve immediately.

Pasta with Ricotta and Arugula

SERVES 6

The peppery, bitter flavor of arugula balances deliciously with the sweet flavor of ricotta cheese and basil in this colorful pasta dish.

1 **pound farfalle pasta (bow ties)**
3 **tablespoons extra virgin olive oil**
4 **large cloves garlic, coarsely chopped**
1 **small yellow onion, finely chopped**
3 **ripe large tomatoes, coarsely chopped, including juices**
6 **large fresh basil leaves**
   Salt and pepper to taste
2 **large bunches arugula (about 1¹/₄ pounds), bottom 2 inches of stem trimmed off**
1 **pound ricotta cheese**
¹/₄ **cup grated Parmigiano-Reggiano cheese**

1. Bring a stockpot of lightly salted water to a boil over high heat and cook the farfalle according to package directions. Before draining the pasta, reserve 1 cup of the cooking water.

2. Meanwhile, heat the oil in a large pot over medium heat. Add the garlic, onion, tomatoes, and basil. Sprinkle with salt and pepper. Cover and cook, stirring occasionally, for 15 minutes, or until the tomatoes release some of their juices and soften. Add the arugula and stir to coat with the juices. Cover and cook for 10 minutes, stirring occasionally.

3. Stir in the ricotta, Parmigiano-Reggiano, and reserved pasta cooking water. Stir well for 1 to 2 minutes to combine the ingredients and heat the ricotta.

4. Add the cooked farfalle and toss well to coat evenly. Cook, uncovered, stirring frequently, for 2 to 3 minutes, or until the sauce reduces slightly. Taste for seasonings.

Semolina Gnocchi

SERVES 6

Every Italian family has its favorite types of gnocchi. My family makes the dumplings with potato, ricotta, or pumpkin, and recently we added semolina. Semolina flour, milled from hard durum wheat, is available in most supermarkets. Many people serve these gnocchi with a butter and sage sauce, but I prefer them baked over a basil-scented marinara sauce with grated pecorino Romano cheese on top.

Note: As the semolina flour boils in the water, it may spout out boiling liquid, so please be careful. I wear either long sleeves and oven mitts or really long oven mitts while whisking the mixture.

> **9 cups water**
> **3 cups semolina flour**
> **4 cups Basil-Scented Marinara Sauce (page 150)**
> **$1/2$ cup grated pecorino Romano cheese**

1. Spray a large rimmed cookie sheet or jelly-roll pan with nonstick cooking spray.

2. Bring the water to a rolling boil in a stockpot over high heat. Using a long whisk, begin whisking the water in a circular motion. Continue whisking while you add the flour $1/2$ cup at a time. When you have whisked in all of the flour, lower the heat to medium and continue whisking for 1 minute, or until the mixture thickens. The mixture will bubble up as it boils, so be careful to avoid spatters. Immediately spread the mixture onto the prepared cookie sheet, using a rubber spatula to scrape the pot clean and to smooth the top. Set aside for about $1^{1}/2$ hours, or until it is firm to the touch (or you can cover the pan and refrigerate the mixture overnight).

3. Preheat the oven to 350 degrees. Spray a 13×9-inch glass baking dish with nonstick cooking spray. Spoon 2 cups of the marinara sauce into the dish. Using a heavy shot glass or $3^{1}/2$-inch cookie cutter, cut out rounds from the dough. As you cut the rounds, arrange them over the sauce, overlapping slightly. Spoon the remaining 2 cups of marinara sauce evenly over the gnocchi. Sprinkle the grated cheese evenly on top.

4. Bake for about 1 hour, or until the sauce is bubbling and the gnocchi are heated through. Test the gnocchi by inserting a butter knife into the center of one. If the knife is hot when you remove it, the gnocchi are heated through. Serve immediately. Leftovers reheat beautifully.

Orecchiette with Kidney Bean Sauce

SERVES 6

I rediscovered orecchiette pasta on a recent trip to Amalfi. The "little ears" of this particular pasta make ideal cups for a delicious sauce of kidney beans and tomato.

Note: Dried beans are now available in 14- or 16-ounce packages. The sizes are interchangeable in any of my recipes.

- 3 quarts water
- 1 (14-ounce) package dried kidney beans, picked over
- 2 large bay leaves
- 1/4 cup extra virgin olive oil
- 6 large cloves garlic, cut into thick slices
- 1 medium yellow onion, finely chopped
  Salt and pepper to taste
- 1 (6-ounce) can tomato paste
- 4 large fresh basil leaves
- 1/2 cup coarsely chopped flat-leaf parsley
- 1 pound orecchiette pasta, cooked according to package directions

1. Place the water, kidney beans, and bay leaves in a large pot, cover, and bring to a boil over high heat. Lower the heat to medium. Cook at a medium boil, stirring occasionally, for about 1 1/2 hours, or until the beans are barely tender.

2. Heat the oil in a large skillet over medium heat. Add the garlic, onion, salt, and pepper. Stir to mix. Cook, stirring occasionally, for about 5 minutes, or until the onions and garlic are light brown but not burned. Add the tomato paste, basil, and parsley, stirring well to mix. Cook for 2 minutes, stirring frequently.

3. Turn the onion mixture into the pot of beans, using a rubber spatula to scrape the skillet clean. Stir well to combine. Continue cooking at a medium boil, stirring occasionally, for 20 minutes, or until the beans are soft and the sauce is thickened.

4. Stir in the cooked orecchiette. Taste for seasonings. Serve with additional pepper on top if desired.

Penne with Sicilian Eggplant, Cherry Tomatoes, Leeks, and Peperoncini

SERVES 6

Sicilian eggplants have a beautiful garnet purple skin and a sweet, creamy flesh. They are usually round in shape, although they do become elongated if left to grow larger. Sicilian eggplant can be used in any recipe that calls for this vegetable.

Note: Ricotta salata is a semifirm Italian cheese with a nutty flavor. It is available in many supermarkets, sometimes sold as ricotta pecorino.

   1 large Sicilian eggplant (about 2 pounds), cut into $1/2$-inch cubes
      Salt and pepper to taste
   1 pound penne pasta
 $1/4$ cup extra virgin olive oil
   2 medium leeks, white and pale green parts only, well washed and
      coarsely chopped
   3 large cloves garlic, cut into thick slices
  20 large ripe cherry tomatoes (about $1 1/4$ pounds), cut in half
 $1/2$ cup dry red wine (Chianti or other)
   2 tablespoons capers, drained
  10 medium peperoncini, drained
 $1/4$ cup finely chopped flat-leaf parsley
   1 tablespoon finely chopped fresh oregano or $1/2$ teaspoon dried
   4 ounces ricotta salata cheese, cut into tiny cubes

1. Place the eggplant in a bowl. Sprinkle generously with salt and pepper and toss to coat. Drain the eggplant in a colander. Let purge for 10 minutes or so.

2. Bring a stockpot of lightly salted water to boil over high heat and cook the penne according to package directions. Before draining the pasta, reserve 1 cup of the cooking water.

3. Meanwhile, heat the olive oil in a large, deep skillet over medium heat. Add the eggplant, leeks, garlic, and cherry tomatoes to the skillet. Cover and cook, stirring occasionally, for 10 minutes, or until the eggplant is barely tender. Add the wine, reserved pasta cooking water, capers, peperoncini, parsley, and oregano. Cover and cook for 10 minutes, stirring occasionally.

4. Add the cooked penne and toss well to combine. Scatter the cheese evenly over the pasta. Stir to mix in. Serve immediately.

Penne with Creamy Mushroom and Vodka Sauce

SERVES 6

This luscious, rich sauce is quick enough to prepare for a weeknight supper and elegant enough to serve to special guests.

> 4 tablespoons butter or soybean margarine ($1/2$ stick), cut into 4 pieces
> 1 large shallot, finely chopped
> 1 large clove garlic, finely chopped
> 1 pound assorted mushrooms (button, shiitake, oyster, and portobello), cut into thick slices
> Salt and pepper to taste
> 1 pound penne pasta
> 1 pint cherry tomatoes (about 20 large), cut into halves
> $1/4$ cup vodka
> $1/2$ teaspoon red pepper flakes
> 3 cups milk or soy milk
> 3 tablespoons unbleached all-purpose flour
> $1/2$ cup grated Parmigiano-Reggiano cheese (optional)

1. Melt the butter in a large pot over medium-low heat. Add the shallot and garlic. Cover and cook, stirring occasionally, for 2 minutes, or until the shallot is softened. Add the mushrooms, salt, and pepper. Cover and cook, stirring occasionally, for 10 minutes, or until the mushrooms have released some of their moisture.

2. Meanwhile, bring a stockpot of lightly salted water to a boil over high heat and cook the penne according to package directions. Before draining the pasta, reserve 1 cup of the cooking water.

3. Add the cherry tomatoes, vodka, and red pepper flakes to the mushrooms. Stir well to mix. Raise the heat to medium and bring to a medium boil. Cover and cook for about 10 minutes, stirring occasionally.

4. Combine the milk and flour in a bowl and whisk to blend. Stir into the mushroom mixture. Cover and cook, stirring frequently, for 8 to 10 minutes, or until the sauce thickens slightly.

5. Add the reserved cooking water and the cooked penne. Toss well to coat the pasta evenly. Cook for 1 minute, stirring frequently. Stir in the grated cheese if desired. Taste for seasonings.

Penne with Creamy Tomato-Vegetable Sauce

SERVES 6

You'll love the interesting flavor combination of sweet and salty in this sauce made with fresh vegetables, sun-dried tomatoes, artichoke hearts, and olives. And the soy milk and Romano cheese stirred in at the end add a dimension of richness and creaminess.

- 2 medium carrots, peeled and cut into julienne pieces
- 2 cups broccoli florets, broken into small pieces
- 1/4 cup extra virgin olive oil
- 4 large cloves garlic, cut into thin slices
- 5 ripe large tomatoes, chopped, including juices
- 1 large bay leaf
- 1 teaspoon red pepper flakes
- 1/2 cup dry white wine
- 10 large fresh basil leaves
  Salt and pepper to taste
- 1 pound penne pasta
- 1 (10-ounce) bag spinach, well washed, drained, and coarsely chopped
- 1 (14-ounce) can artichoke hearts, drained and cut into thick slices
- 1/8 teaspoon ground red pepper
- 1/4 cup oil-cured black olives
- 12 large green olives
- 2 tablespoons drained and finely chopped sun-dried tomatoes in oil
- 1/2 cup milk or soy milk
- 1/2 cup grated pecorino Romano cheese

1. Bring a covered pot of lightly salted water to a boil over high heat. Add the carrots and broccoli florets, cover, and cook for 1 minute. Using a slotted spoon, transfer the cooked vegetables to a bowl. Reserve the water for cooking the pasta.

2. Heat the oil in a large pot over medium heat. Add the garlic and tomatoes and stir to coat with the oil. Cover and cook, stirring occasionally, for 25 minutes, or until the tomatoes release some of their juices. Add the bay leaf, red pepper flakes, wine, basil leaves, salt, and pepper. Cover and cook at a medium boil for 10 minutes, stirring occasionally.

3. Meanwhile, begin to cook the penne according to package directions.

4. Add the spinach, artichoke hearts, red pepper, olives, and sun-dried tomatoes to the sauce. Stir to mix. Cover and cook for 5 minutes, stirring occasionally. Stir in the milk, cooked penne, broccoli, carrots, and cheese. Stir to coat the pasta with the sauce. Taste for seasonings.

Homemade Manicotti

MAKES ABOUT 24

My mother-in-law makes the tenderest pasta crepes, known as crespelle *in Italian. She fills them with a mixture of ricotta, Parmigiano-Reggiano, and mozzarella, then bakes them in her Basil-Scented Marinara Sauce (page 150). In our family we traditionally serve homemade manicotti (or Holiday Lasagne, page 144) on Christmas and Easter.*

Pasta Crepes:
- 2 **cups unbleached all-purpose flour**
- 4 **eggs**
- 2 **cups water**
-    **Salt and pepper to taste**

Filling:
- 2 **pounds ricotta cheese**
- 2 **eggs**
- 2 **tablespoons finely chopped flat-leaf parsley**
- 1/4 **cup grated Parmigiano-Reggiano cheese**
- 4 **ounces mozzarella cheese, grated**
-    **Salt and pepper to taste**

4 **cups Basil-Scented Marinara Sauce (page 150)**

1. To prepare the pasta crepes, measure the flour into a bowl. In a separate bowl, whisk the eggs, water, salt, and pepper. Pour this mixture all at once over the flour. Mix well with a fork or whisk until the batter is smooth. Set aside while you prepare the filling.

2. Combine all the filling ingredients in a bowl. Beat the ingredients with a spoon until well combined. Cover and refrigerate while you cook the pasta crepes.

3. Line a cookie sheet with wax paper and set it by the stove. Spray a small non-stick skillet with cooking spray. Heat the skillet over medium heat. Stir the pasta crepe batter. Spoon about 3 tablespoons of the batter into the center of the heated skillet, tilting the pan to coat the bottom. Cook for 25 to 30 seconds, or until the crepe is set. Carefully turn the crepe and cook the other side for 10 to 15 seconds, or until the crepe no longer looks wet. Transfer the cooked crepe to the lined cookie sheet. Repeat the process with the remaining batter. Transfer the cooked crepes, overlapping slightly, onto the cookie sheet as you cook them.

4. Preheat the oven to 400 degrees. Spoon 1 cup of marinara sauce into a 13 × 9-inch glass baking dish. Lay a crepe on your hand and spoon 2 to 3 tablespoons of the filling in the center. Fold each side of the crepe over to encase the filling. Place the filled manicotti, seam side down, in the baking dish. Fill the remaining pasta crepes and arrange them in a single layer in the dish. Spoon the remaining marinara sauce evenly over the manicotti. Bake for about 30 minutes, or until the sauce is hot and bubbling, and the manicotti are warm inside when tested with a fork (insert a fork into the center of a manicotti; if the tines are hot when you remove the fork, the filling is ready). Serve immediately; refrigerate leftovers.

Linguine with Pumpkin Sauce

SERVES 6

This recipe is our family's traditional fall favorite. It uses deep orange-colored pumpkin squash rather than the pumpkin usually used for pumpkin pies. Pumpkin squash are available in the fall in Italian markets and most supermarkets. You can substitute calabaza squash, which is sold in chunks cut from this huge West Indian member of the squash family. While the flavor is a little milder than that of Italian pumpkin squash, the sauce will still be delicious.

- 1/4 cup extra virgin olive oil
- 4 large cloves garlic, coarsely chopped
- 2 pounds pumpkin squash, peeled and cut into 1-inch cubes
- 1 large sweet onion, cut into thick ribs
- 1/4 cup fresh basil leaves
- 1/2 cup coarsely chopped flat-leaf parsley
  Salt and pepper to taste
- 1 pound linguine
- 1/8 teaspoon ground nutmeg
- 1/4 cup lightly toasted pumpkin seeds (optional)

1. Heat the oil in a large pot over medium-low heat. Add the garlic, squash, onion, basil, parsley, salt, and pepper. Stir to coat with the oil. Cover and cook, stirring occasionally, for about 25 minutes, or until the squash is just tender and has released some of its moisture.

2. Meanwhile, bring a stockpot of lightly salted water to a boil over high heat and cook the linguine according to package directions. Before draining the linguine, reserve 2 cups of the cooking water.

3. When the squash is just tender, add the reserved pasta cooking water and the nutmeg. Stir well to mix. Cover and cook for about 5 minutes, stirring occasionally. Taste for seasonings. Add the cooked linguine to the pot and toss well. Taste for seasonings. Turn into a serving bowl. Top with the toasted pumpkin seeds if desired.

Farfalle with Spinach, Tomatoes, and Wine

SERVES 6

My brother Paul came up with this recipe during one of his culinary experiences in a New Haven restaurant years ago. It is the essence of simplicity and memorable flavor.

1 pound farfalle pasta (bow ties)
1/4 cup extra virgin olive oil
1 large shallot, finely chopped
2 large cloves garlic, coarsely chopped
1 large yellow onion, coarsely chopped
5 ripe large tomatoes, coarsely chopped, including juices
    Salt and pepper to taste
1/2 cup dry white wine
5 large fresh basil leaves
1 (10-ounce) bag spinach, well washed, drained, and coarsely chopped

1. Put a stockpot of lightly salted water to a boil over high heat and cook the farfalle according to package directions. Before draining the pasta, reserve 2 cups of the cooking water.

2. Meanwhile, heat the oil in a large pot over medium heat. Add the shallot, garlic, onion, tomatoes, salt, and pepper. Stir to coat with the oil. Cover and cook, stirring occasionally, for 20 minutes, or until the tomatoes are soft.

3. Add the wine, basil, and spinach to the tomato mixture. Stir well to mix. Cover and cook, stirring occasionally, for 5 minutes, or until the spinach is wilted. Stir in the reserved pasta cooking water and the cooked farfalle. Stir well to combine. Cover and cook for 2 minutes, stirring occasionally. Taste for seasonings. Turn into a serving bowl.

Pastina with Butter and Eggs

SERVES 6

There have been many Saturdays when I've come home, after a particularly busy twelve-hour workday at Claire's, and made this simple dish for supper. I think of it as the ultimate in comfort food.

       2 quarts water
    1³/₄ cups pastina (tiny pasta bits)
          Salt and pepper to taste
       6 eggs
     ¹/₄ cup finely chopped flat-leaf parsley
     ¹/₂ cup grated Parmigiano-Reggiano cheese
       2 tablespoons butter

1. Bring the water to a boil in a large pot over high heat. Stir in the pastina, salt, and pepper. Cook for 4 minutes, stirring occasionally.

2. Meanwhile, combine the eggs, parsley, and cheese in a bowl. Beat to mix with a fork or whisk.

3. After the pasta has cooked, do not drain it. Stir in the butter and continue stirring for about 1 minute, or until it melts. Add the egg mixture. Stir well to combine. Cook, stirring frequently, for 2 minutes, or until the eggs are cooked. Taste for seasonings.

Spaghetti with Cauliflower, Parmigiano, and Eggs

SERVES 6

When Frank and I traveled to southern Italy to visit a cannery that packs San Marzano tomatoes (the sweet, exquisite Italian tomatoes I adore), I met the manager of the cannery and his charming family, who happen to live next door to it. They invited us in for espresso and a tour of their vegetable gardens. They even allowed us up to their roof (their flat roof!), where we had the great fortune to take stunning photographs of the cannery yard. We looked down on acres of crates filled with perfectly ripened, long, crimson red San Marzano tomatoes, destined for export to several countries, with America, fortunately, on that list. During that wonderful afternoon, Elvira, the eldest daughter, who is studying law in Naples, shared this recipe with me.

1 **pound spaghetti**
3 **quarts water**
1 **large head cauliflower**
   Salt and pepper to taste
6 **tablespoons olive oil**
1 **large yellow onion, finely chopped**
6 **eggs**
1 **cup finely chopped flat-leaf parsley**
1/2 **cup grated Parmigiano-Reggiano cheese**

1. Bring a stockpot of lightly salted water to a boil over high heat and cook the spaghetti according to package directions.

2. Meanwhile, bring the 3 quarts of water to a boil in a separate large pot. Add the head of cauliflower along with the green leaves attached to the base. Sprinkle with salt and pepper, cover, and cook for about 10 minutes, or until the cauliflower is fork-tender, occasionally turning it so that it will cook evenly. Drain, reserving the cooking water. When the cauliflower is cool enough to handle, remove and discard the leaves. Place the cauliflower in a bowl and mash it into small pieces.

3. In the pot you used for cooking the spaghetti, heat 4 tablespoons of the oil over medium heat. Add the onion, salt, and pepper. Cook, stirring occasionally, for

2 to 3 minutes, or until the onion is golden brown. Add the cauliflower and 4 cups of the reserved cooking water. Stir well to mix. Cover and cook for 5 minutes, stirring occasionally.

4. Combine the eggs, parsley, and cheese in a bowl and whisk lightly. Add the cooked spaghetti to the cauliflower mixture. Stir to mix. Add the beaten egg mixture, using a rubber spatula to scrape out the bowl. Stir well to combine. Cover and cook, stirring frequently, for 4 to 5 minutes, or until the eggs are cooked. Drizzle the remaining 2 tablespoons oil over the top. Toss to combine. Taste for seasonings.

Spinach and Ricotta Dumplings

SERVES 6

Lydia, a Sicilian woman I met at a workshop in Fort Lauderdale, Florida, many years ago, told me about this luscious and surprisingly light dish. She called them ravioli nudi, *or "nude ravioli." They are delicious dumplings of fresh spinach and ricotta cheese that are poached in boiling water, then baked in marinara sauce.*

> 2 **(10-ounce) bags spinach, well washed and drained**
> 1 **pound ricotta cheese**
> 2 **eggs**
> 1/4 **cup grated Parmigiano-Reggiano cheese**
> 2 1/2 **cups unbleached all-purpose flour**
> 1/8 **teaspoon grated nutmeg**
> **Salt and pepper to taste**
> 4 **cups Basil-Scented Marinara Sauce (page 150)**

1. Place the drained spinach with only the water clinging to its leaves in a pot. Cover and cook over medium-low heat, stirring occasionally, for 8 minutes, or until the spinach is wilted. Drain. When cool enough to handle, squeeze out as much excess water as possible. Finely chop the spinach and place in a bowl. Add the ricotta, eggs, cheese, 2 cups of the flour, the nutmeg, salt, and pepper and mix well. Taste for seasonings.

2. Measure the remaining flour into a pie pan. Using about 3 tablespoons at a time, form the spinach mixture into egg-shaped dumplings. Gently cover each dumpling with the flour, turning to coat. Gently shake off the excess flour and place the coated dumpling on a platter. Continue to form and coat the remaining spinach mixture.

3. Bring a large pot of lightly salted water to a simmer over medium heat. Preheat the oven to 400 degrees. Carefully drop 5 or 6 dumplings at a time into the boiling water. Cook, uncovered, for 10 to 12 minutes, or until they float to the top. Using a slotted spoon, transfer the dumplings to a platter. Cook the remaining dumplings, 5 or 6 at a time in the boiling water.

4. Spread the marinara sauce in a rectangular glass baking dish. Arrange the dumplings over the sauce, then turn each to coat with the sauce. Cover the dish tightly with foil. Bake for about 1 hour, or until the sauce is bubbling.

Tagliatelle with Zucchini, Oyster Mushrooms, Lemon, and Mint

SERVES 6

During a train ride from Sorrento to Naples, I met a young man by the name of Andrew Cook, who was in Italy looking for work as a chef. He was born and raised in Ireland and had spent many years in London working as a chef in a restaurant owned by men from Sorrento. We enjoyed a long conversation during our train ride, and of course, the topic was food. He gave me the idea for this recipe.

- 1 pound tagliatelle pasta or fettuccine
- 1/4 cup extra virgin olive oil
- 2 medium leeks, white and pale green parts only, well washed and coarsely chopped
- 1 large shallot, finely chopped
- 3 small to medium zucchini, diced
- 1 bunch thin asparagus (about 12 ounces), trimmed and cut into 1/2-inch lengths
  Salt and pepper to taste
- 8 ounces oyster mushrooms, separated
- 1/4 cup coarsely chopped fresh mint
- 3 tablespoons white balsamic vinegar
- 3 tablespoons fresh lemon juice (about 1 lemon)

1. Bring a stockpot of lightly salted water to a boil over high heat and cook the tagliatelle according to package directions. Before draining the pasta, reserve 2 cups of the cooking water.

2. Meanwhile, heat the oil in a large pot over medium heat. Add the leeks, shallot, zucchini, asparagus, salt, and pepper. Cover and cook for 10 minutes, stirring occasionally. Add the mushrooms and the mint. Cover and cook, stirring occasionally, for 4 to 5 minutes, or until the mushrooms are tender.

3. Stir in the vinegar, lemon juice, and reserved pasta cooking water. Cover and cook for 2 minutes, stirring occasionally. Add the cooked tagliatelle and toss well to coat the pasta with the broth. Cover and cook for 1 minute, stirring frequently. Taste for seasonings. Serve immediately.

Eggplant Lasagne

SERVES 6

This layered dish of sautéed eggplant cutlets, ground "meat," ricotta, and mozzarella, baked with marinara sauce has become the signature lasagne for my mother-in-law. It is one of the most popular dishes both at my restaurant and in my home.

Note: Meatless ground "beef" is available in health foods stores and in many supermarkets. I mainly use either Ground Meatless by Morningstar Farms or Gimme Lean by Lightlife.

1   **medium eggplant**
    Salt and pepper to taste
3   **tablespoons olive oil**
2   **(1-inch-thick) slices Italian bread**
1   **(14-ounce) package meatless ground "beef"**
1/4 **cup finely chopped flat-leaf parsley**
2   **small yellow onions, finely chopped**
3   **large cloves garlic, finely chopped**
3   **eggs**
1   **pound ricotta cheese**
8   **ounces mozzarella cheese, shredded**
1/4 **cup grated Parmigiano-Reggiano cheese**
1   **(28-ounce) can Italian whole peeled tomatoes in juice, squeezed with your hands to crush**
1   **teaspoon dried oregano**

1. Trim the eggplant. Cut into 1/4-inch-thick rounds. Sprinkle both sides of the slices with salt and pepper. Heat 1 tablespoon of the oil in a large nonstick skillet over medium heat. Cook the eggplant slices for about 2 minutes on each side, or until just softened. Set aside.

2. Place the slices of bread in a bowl. Cover with hot tap water. When cool enough to handle, turn into a colander. Squeeze out as much water as you can, pressing the bread against the colander. Turn into a bowl. Add the ground "beef,"

2 tablespoons of the parsley, half of the chopped onions, one-third of the chopped garlic, one of the eggs, and salt and pepper. Using your hands or a spoon, mix well.

3. In a separate bowl, combine the ricotta, the remaining 2 eggs, the cheeses, and salt and pepper. Stir to mix well.

4. In a separate bowl, combine the tomatoes, the remaining 2 tablespoons oil, the remaining chopped onion, the remaining garlic, the remaining 2 tablespoons parsley, the oregano, and salt and pepper. Stir the mixture to combine.

5. Preheat the oven to 400 degrees. Spray a 3-quart glass casserole dish with nonstick cooking spray. Arrange the eggplant slices in the bottom and up the sides of the dish. Spoon the "beef" mixture evenly over the eggplant. Spoon the ricotta mixture evenly over the "beef." Spoon the tomato mixture evenly over the top. Cover the dish tightly with foil. Bake for about 1 1/2 hours, or until the eggplant is tender when tested with a fork.

Holiday Lasagne

SERVES 8

Every holiday for as far back as I can remember has included this special lasagne made with tiny meatballs (meatless balls today), sliced hard-cooked eggs, ricotta, mozzarella and Parmigiano-Reggiano cheeses, and a smooth marinara sauce, encased in layers of lasagne noodles. Together, my mom and I rolled what seemed like hundreds of marble-size meatballs while sitting at the kitchen table, just laughing and talking.

Note: I use Gimme Lean beef flavor in this recipe.

Meatless Balls:
  1 (14-ounce) package meatless ground "beef"
  1/2 cup plain dry bread crumbs
  3 tablespoons finely chopped flat-leaf parsley
  1 large clove garlic, finely chopped
  2 eggs
      Salt and pepper to taste

Ricotta Filling:
  1 pound ricotta cheese
  2 eggs
  1/4 cup grated Parmigiano-Reggiano cheese
  4 ounces shredded mozzarella cheese
  3 tablespoons finely chopped flat-leaf parsley
      Salt and pepper to taste

For the Assembly:
  1 pound lasagne noodles
  5 cups Holiday Marinara Sauce (page 148)
  2 hard-cooked eggs, sliced
  4 ounces mozzarella cheese, shredded

1. Preheat the oven to 350 degrees. Spray a cookie sheet with olive oil cooking spray. Place all the ingredients for the meatless balls in a bowl. Mix well with your hands or a spoon. Using about 1 teaspoonful at a time, roll the mixture into about

45 little balls. Arrange them on the prepared cookie sheet. Bake for 20 minutes, or until the "meatballs" are just firm to the touch. Remove from the oven, but leave the oven on to bake the lasagne.

2. Cook the lasagne noodles according to package directions. Meanwhile, place all the ricotta filling ingredients in a bowl and mix well.

3. To assemble the lasagne, spread a thin layer of marinara sauce on the bottom of a 13 × 9-inch baking pan. Place a single layer of lasagne noodles in the pan, overlapping slightly. Spread one-third of the ricotta filling over the noodles. Scatter one-third of the "meatballs" evenly over the ricotta. Scatter one-third of the sliced hard-cooked eggs and one-third of the remaining mozzarella over the top. Spoon a thin layer of marinara sauce over the top.

4. Repeat the layers, but this time arrange the lasagne noodles in the crosswise direction from the first layer (this will make serving easier), trimming as necessary. Add a third layer, using the remaining ricotta filling, "meatballs," mozzarella cheese, and hard-cooked eggs. Finish with a layer of lasagne noodles and spread marinara sauce on top.

5. This dish can be prepared 1 day in advance. Cover with plastic wrap (not foil, because the acid from the marinara sauce can cause little bits of foil to get into the sauce) and refrigerate. When ready to bake, remove the plastic wrap. Bake for 45 minutes. Let stand about 15 minutes before serving.

Ricotta Gnocchi

SERVES 8

These little ricotta dumplings melt in your mouth. Cover them with marinara sauce and serve with Sautéed Spinach (page 54) and Salad from Sorrento (page 92) for a traditional Italian Sunday dinner.

> 5 cups unbleached all-purpose flour
> 2 pounds ricotta cheese
> 1/2 cup grated Parmigiano-Reggiano cheese
> 2 tablespoons finely minced flat-leaf parsley
> 2 eggs, lightly beaten
> Salt and pepper to taste
> 4 cups Basil-Scented Marinara Sauce (page 150)

1. Measure 4 1/2 cups of the flour into a large bowl. Add the ricotta, Parmigiano, parsley, eggs, salt, and pepper. Mix well to combine.

2. Scatter 2 to 3 tablespoons of flour on a large wooden cutting board or the countertop. Place the ricotta dough on the board and knead it for about 10 minutes, working in 2 to 3 tablespoons of additional flour at a time.

3. When the dough is smooth, roll it into a 16-inch-long log. Set 2 cookie sheets nearby. Dust them lightly with 1 to 2 tablespoons of flour. Cut 2-inch-thick slices from the dough. Roll each slice into a 16-inch-long rope. Cut the rope into 1-inch pieces. Place the pieces in a single layer on the cookie sheets. Continue cutting and rolling the remaining dough.

4. Bring 2 large pots of lightly salted water to a boil over high heat. Add half of the dough pieces to each pot of boiling water and cook, stirring occasionally with a wooden spoon, for about 5 minutes, or until the gnocchi are tender and float to the surface. Drain.

5. Heat the marinara sauce in a large pot. Add the drained gnocchi. Stir to coat. Turn into a serving bowl.

Spaghetti with Olive Oil, Garlic Chips, and Capers

SERVES 6

Olive oil and garlic (in Italian, aglio e olio) *tossed with spaghetti is the quintessential Friday night meal in an Italian home. This is a holdover from the time when most Italian Catholics abstained from eating meat on Friday. In my house we are happy to eat this pasta dish on any night.*

- **1 pound thin spaghetti**
- **1/4 cup extra virgin olive oil**
- **10 large cloves garlic, cut lengthwise into thick slices**
- **2 tablespoons capers, drained**
- **1/2 teaspoon red pepper flakes**
- **Salt and pepper to taste**

1. Bring a stockpot of lightly salted water to a boil over high heat and cook the spaghetti according to package directions. Before draining the spaghetti, reserve 2 cups of the cooking water.

2. Heat the oil in a large skillet over medium-low heat. Add the garlic and cook, stirring occasionally, for 2 to 3 minutes, until the garlic is golden brown but not burned. Add the capers, red pepper flakes, reserved pasta cooking water, salt, and pepper. Cook at a medium boil for 2 minutes, stirring frequently. Add the cooked spaghetti and toss to mix well. Taste for seasonings. Serve immediately.

Holiday Marinara Sauce

MAKES ABOUT 5 1/2 QUARTS

The holiday table in our family always includes a special pasta dish such as Holiday Lasagne (page 144) or Homemade Manicotti (page 132). In addition, our holiday antipasto platters include items that are traditionally served with marinara sauce. Therefore, we usually prepare a pot of sauce big enough for the feast ahead.

$3/4$ **cup olive oil**
2 **large yellow onions, coarsely chopped**
10 **large cloves garlic, coarsely chopped**
2 **(6-ounce) cans tomato paste**
4 **(28-ounce) cans crushed Italian tomatoes**
3 **large bay leaves**
$1/2$ **teaspoon red pepper flakes**
1 **cup finely chopped flat-leaf parsley**
2 **quarts water**
$1/2$ **cup fresh basil leaves**
   Salt and pepper to taste

1. Heat the oil in a stockpot over medium heat. Add the onions and garlic. Cook, stirring occasionally, for about 30 minutes, or until the onions are a deep golden brown but not burned. Add the tomato paste. Stir well to blend. Cook for 2 minutes, stirring frequently.

2. Add the crushed tomatoes, bay leaves, red pepper flakes, parsley, water, basil, salt, and pepper. Raise the heat to medium-high. Cover and bring to a medium boil (this should take about 20 minutes), stirring occasionally. Lower the heat to medium-low. Cook, uncovered, stirring occasionally, for 45 minutes, or until the sauce has reduced by about one-quarter. Taste for seasonings.

Fresh Tomato Sauce

MAKES ABOUT 6 CUPS

This quick sauce is perfect for the summer months. Use ripe plum tomatoes to make a delicious sauce for pasta, pizza, or rice.

  3 **tablespoons extra virgin olive oil**
  4 **large cloves garlic, cut into thin slices**
  1 **medium red onion, finely chopped**
24 **ripe plum tomatoes, coarsely chopped, including juices**
  3 **tablespoons finely chopped flat-leaf parsley**
  5 **large fresh basil leaves, coarsely chopped**
  5 **medium fresh sage leaves, finely chopped, or 1 teaspoon dried sage**
  3 **tablespoons dry white wine**
     Salt and pepper to taste

Heat the oil in a large skillet over medium-high heat. Add the remaining ingredients and stir to mix. Cover and bring to a medium boil, then lower the heat to medium and cook, stirring occasionally, for about 20 minutes, or until the sauce reduces by about half. Taste for seasonings.

Basil~Scented Marinara Sauce

MAKES ABOUT 5 CUPS (PLENTY FOR 1 POUND OF PASTA)

I enjoy a good marinara sauce more than any other, and this one is perfect for fettuccine.

- 3 tablespoons extra virgin olive oil
- 6 large cloves garlic, cut into thick slices
- 1 small yellow onion, finely chopped
- 1 (35-ounce) can Italian whole peeled tomatoes in juice, squeezed with your hands to crush
- 1/2 cup dry red wine
- 10 large fresh basil leaves
- 1/4 cup coarsely chopped flat-leaf parsley
- 2 bay leaves
  Salt and pepper to taste

Heat the oil in a large pot over medium heat. Add the garlic and onion. Cover and cook, stirring occasionally, for 7 to 10 minutes, or until the garlic and onion are light brown but not burned. Add the remaining ingredients and stir well to mix. Cover and cook at a medium boil (this should take about 5 minutes), stirring occasionally, for about 20 minutes, or until the sauce reduces slightly. Taste for seasonings.

Entrees

Zucchini Parmigiana
Squash Blossom Pancakes
Giambotto
Potato and Onion Frittata
Cannellini Baked with Sausage and Bacon
Cannellini and Swiss Chard over Tomato-Onion Polenta
Sorrentina Spinach and Semolina
Spinach Patties
Cornmeal Loaves with Raisins and Fennel Seeds
Pizza Amalfitan Style
Pizza Fritti
Potato and Sausage Pizza
Pizza Fritti Stuffed with Escarole and "Pepperoni"
Tomato Bread
Fresh Mozzarella in Bread
Fried Mozzarella Cheese
Swiss Chard Calzone
Spinach Risotto
Risotto with Smoked Mozzarella and Green Peas
Artichoke Hearts in Marinara Sauce with Rice and Peas
Stewed Zucchini and Tomatoes over Arborio Rice

Stuffed Zucchini

Stuffed Fryers

Red Bell Peppers Stuffed with Arborio Rice and Artichoke Hearts

Red Bell Peppers Stuffed with Mashed Potatoes

Stuffed Onions

Stuffed Portobello Mushrooms

Pan-Seared Herb-Crusted Portobello Mushrooms

Portobello Mushrooms with Cannellini Beans

Italian Hamburgers

Vegetarian Meat Loaf with Roasted White and Sweet Potatoes, Onions, and Carrots

Green Bean, Tomato, Potato, and Meatball Stew

Meatless Italian Sausages Roasted with Mushrooms, Onions, Potatoes, and Peas

Sausage and Pepper Rolls

Sausage Pizzaiola Style

Pastina and Sausage Pie

Broccoli Rabe and Sausage Pinwheel Bread

Seitan

Seitan Milanese

Seitan Francese

Seitan Scarpariello

Fava Beans and Smothered Onions over Seitan

Zucchini Parmigiana

SERVES 4

Enjoy this quintessential southern Italian favorite with a simple salad for dinner, or serve it with pasta and marinara sauce for a little more substantial meal. Any leftovers make a terrific sandwich filling in Italian bread.

3 **medium to large zucchini (about 2¹/₂ pounds), cut lengthwise into ¹/₄-inch-thick slices**
  Salt and pepper to taste
1 **cup unbleached all-purpose flour**
6 **eggs**
¹/₄ **cup finely chopped flat-leaf parsley**
¹/₂ **cup olive oil**
4 **cups Basil-Scented Marinara Sauce (page 150)**
¹/₄ **cup grated Parmigiano-Reggiano cheese**
4 **ounces mozzarella cheese, grated**

1. Line a cookie sheet with a double layer of paper towels and set it next to the stove. Sprinkle the zucchini slices with salt and pepper. Measure the flour into a shallow bowl. Break the eggs into a second shallow bowl. Add the parsley, salt, and pepper and beat lightly with a fork or a whisk.

2. Heat ¹/₄ cup of the oil in a large skillet over medium heat. Working quickly, dredge a zucchini slice in the flour, turning to coat both sides. Shake off the excess flour. Dip the slice into the beaten eggs, using a fork to turn the slice to coat both sides. Shake off the excess. Place the zucchini slice in the heated oil. Repeat until you have as many zucchini slices in the skillet as will fit in a single layer (do not over-crowd, or the oil temperature will drop and the zucchini will be greasy).

3. Cook the zucchini for about 3 minutes, or until golden brown on the under-side. Turn the slices and cook the other side for about 2 minutes, or until golden brown. Transfer the cooked slices to the towel-lined cookie sheet. Repeat with the remaining zucchini slices, heating additional oil as needed.

4. Preheat the oven to 375 degrees. Spoon 1 cup of the marinara sauce evenly in a 13 × 9-inch glass baking dish. Arrange a layer of cooked zucchini slices over the sauce. Spoon 1 cup of the marinara sauce over the zucchini. Sprinkle a little of each of the cheeses evenly on top. Add another layer of zucchini slices, sauce, and each of the cheeses and continue layering until all the ingredients are used. Bake for about 1 hour, or until the sauce is hot and bubbling.

Squash Blossom Pancakes

SERVES 6 (MAKES ABOUT 32 PANCAKES)

Every summer my grandfather and I would pick the blossoms from the zucchini in his garden and bring them to Grandma. She and I would prepare these light and delicious pancakes. Today when I make them either in the restaurant or at home, I am transported right back to Grandma's kitchen.

Note: Farm stands will have squash blossoms during the summer.

- 2 **cups unbleached all-purpose flour**
- 2 **teaspoons baking powder**
- 3 **eggs**
- 1 **cup water**
- 8 **to 10 squash blossoms, rinsed and coarsely chopped**
- $1/4$ **cup finely chopped flat-leaf parsley**
- **Salt and pepper to taste**
- $1/2$ **cup olive oil**

1. Measure the flour and baking powder into a large bowl. Stir to combine. In a separate bowl, whisk together the eggs and water. Add the egg mixture to the flour mixture all at once, using a rubber spatula to scrape out the bowl. Stir to combine.

2. Add the squash blossoms, parsley, salt, and pepper to the batter. Stir well to combine.

3. Line a cookie sheet with a double layer of paper towels and set it by the stove. Heat 3 tablespoons of the oil in a large nonstick skillet over medium heat. Drop heaping teaspoons of the batter into the hot oil, fitting as many as you can without crowding. Cook for 2 to 3 minutes, or until the undersides are medium golden brown. Turn and cook the other sides for about 2 minutes, or until medium golden brown. Transfer to the towel-lined cookie sheet.

4. Continue frying the remaining batter, heating additional oil as needed. Serve hot, at room temperature, or chilled.

Giambotto

SERVES 6

My mom referred to any combination of vegetables that she combined in a dish as giambotto. Serve it for dinner with rice and a tossed salad topped with chickpeas.

    3 medium baking potatoes, peeled and cut into quarters
    2 medium eggplants (about 1½ pounds), unpeeled, cut into 1-inch cubes
      Salt and pepper to taste
    3 tablespoons olive oil
    3 ribs celery, cut into ½-inch-thick slices, including leaves
    1 large yellow onion, cut into thick ribs
    3 large cloves garlic, coarsely chopped
    2 medium red or green bell peppers, seeded and cut into thick ribs
¼ cup tomato paste
    2 cups water
    1 teaspoon dried oregano

1. Bring a large pot of lightly salted water to a boil over high heat. Add the potatoes and cook for 12 to 15 minutes, or until fork tender. Drain.

2. Meanwhile, place the eggplants in a bowl. Sprinkle lightly with salt and pepper and toss well to coat.

3. Heat the oil in a large pot over medium-low heat. Add the celery, onion, garlic, peppers, and eggplants. Cover and cook, stirring occasionally, for about 15 minutes, or until the vegetables have softened and released some of their moisture.

4. Add the tomato paste, water, and oregano. Stir well to combine. Cover and cook, stirring occasionally, for about 15 minutes, or until the eggplants and celery are tender. Add the cooked potatoes. Stir to combine. Taste for seasonings.

Potato and Onion Frittata

SERVES 4 TO 6

Italian omelettes, or frittatas, can be cooked on top of the stove or, as in this case, baked in the oven. They make a fine supper when served with a simple salad and good Italian bread. When chilled, leftovers are scrumptious, in a sandwich on Italian bread.

 3 medium potatoes, peeled and cut into $1/4$-inch-thick slices
    Salt and pepper to taste
10 eggs
 1 small yellow onion, finely chopped
$1/4$ cup finely chopped flat-leaf parsley
 4 large fresh basil leaves, coarsely chopped
 1 tablespoon olive oil

1. Preheat the oven to 400 degrees. Bring a large pot of lightly salted water to a boil over high heat. Add the potatoes and cook for 5 to 7 minutes, or until just tender. Drain.

2. In a large bowl, combine the eggs, onion, parsley, basil, salt, and pepper. Beat with a whisk to combine. Stir in the cooked potatoes.

3. Brush a 10-inch pie pan with the oil. Pour the egg mixture into the pan, using a rubber spatula to scrape out the bowl and to smooth the mixture. Bake for 45 to 50 minutes, or until the eggs are set. Cut into wedges and serve.

Cannellini Baked with Sausage and Bacon

SERVES 6

This is my Italian version of the quintessential American baked bean. The protein-rich combination of beans and meatless sausage and bacon makes it an excellent dinner entree. Serve it with corn on the cob and perhaps coleslaw for an Italian American picnic.

1 pound dried cannellini, picked over
1 bay leaf
1 (28-ounce) can crushed Italian tomatoes
1 cup water
2 tablespoons olive oil
1/4 cup coarsely chopped flat-leaf parsley
1 large yellow onion, finely chopped
4 strips meatless bacon, cut into 1-inch pieces
2 large cloves garlic, finely chopped
4 links Italian-style meatless sausage, finely chopped
Salt and pepper to taste

1. Place the cannellini and bay leaf in a large pot and add water to cover by 3 inches. Bring to a boil over high heat, then lower the heat to medium and cook, covered, for 1 to 1 1/2 hours, or until the beans are barely tender. Drain.

2. Preheat the oven to 400 degrees. Turn the cooked beans into a large bowl. Add the remaining ingredients. Stir to mix well. Taste for seasonings.

3. Spray a 4-quart casserole dish with nonstick cooking spray. Turn the bean mixture into the prepared casserole dish, using a rubber spatula to scrape out the bowl. Bake, stirring occasionally, for about 2 hours, or until the beans are tender.

Cannellini and Swiss Chard over Tomato~Onion Polenta

SERVES 6

This colorful dish has a lot of flexibility. You can eat the cannellini and Swiss chard topping as a stew with toasted Italian bread (crostini) and a little grated Parmigiano-Reggiano cheese on top. Also, the tomato-onion polenta is delicious as an entree topped with Basil-Scented Marinara Sauce (page 150) and grated cheese, or as a side dish. Enjoy either or both.

1   pound dried cannellini or great northern beans, picked over
1   large bay leaf
3   tablespoons extra virgin olive oil
3   large cloves garlic, coarsely chopped
1   large bunch Swiss chard, well washed, bottom 6 inches of stem
      trimmed off, and leaves and tender stems cut into 2-inch pieces
3   ripe large tomatoes, coarsely chopped, including juices
      Salt and pepper to taste

Polenta:
8   cups water
1   large yellow onion, coarsely chopped
2   tablespoons tomato paste
      Salt and pepper to taste
2   cups coarse cornmeal
1/2 cup grated Parmigiano-Reggiano cheese

1. Place the cannellini and bay leaf in a large pot and add water to cover by 3 inches. Bring to a boil over high heat, then lower the heat to medium and cook, covered, stirring occasionally, for about $1^1/_2$ hours, or until the beans are soft-tender. Drain.

2. Heat the oil in a large skillet over medium-low heat. Add the garlic, chard, tomatoes, salt, and pepper. Cover and cook, turning with tongs occasionally, for 25 minutes, or until the chard is tender. Add the drained beans to the tomatoes and chard. Stir to mix. Taste for seasonings. Lower the heat to warm. Cover and keep warm while you prepare the polenta.

3. Place the water, onion, tomato paste, salt, and pepper in a large pot. Cover and bring to a boil over high heat. Cook at a boil for 5 minutes, stirring occasionally. Wear oven mitts to protect your hands while you continue.

4. Using a whisk, begin to stir the boiling water in a circular motion. Gradually pour the cornmeal in a steady stream into the boiling water while you whisk continuously. Lower the heat to medium and cook at a medium-low boil, whisking constantly, for 3 to 4 minutes, or until the mixture has thickened. Turn the polenta into a large serving bowl or deep platter. Spoon the cannellini and Swiss chard mixture evenly over the polenta. Sprinkle the grated cheese on top.

Sorrentina Spinach and Semolina

SERVES 8

In Sorrento I ate at a terrific restaurant that featured the most abundant selection of antipasti I have ever seen. This spinach and semolina dish was one of the most memorable dishes.

    7 cups water
    2 cups milk or soy milk
       Salt and pepper to taste
    2 cups semolina flour
    2 (10-ounce) bags spinach, well washed, drained, and finely chopped
    5 large basil leaves, finely chopped
 $1/2$ cup grated Parmigiano-Reggiano cheese
    2 large cloves garlic, finely chopped
    2 eggs
    4 ounces mozzarella cheese, grated
    2 cups Basil-Scented Marinara Sauce (page 150), heated

1. Preheat the oven to 400 degrees. Bring the water, milk, salt, and pepper to a boil in a large covered pot over high heat. Put on oven mitts to protect your hands. Using a whisk, begin to stir the liquid in a circular motion. Whisking continuously, pour the semolina into the boiling liquid in a steady stream. Cook, whisking constantly, for 2 to 3 minutes, or until the mixture has thickened. The mixture will bubble up like a volcano as it cooks—be careful not to get burned. Remove from the heat.

2. Add the spinach and basil, stirring to combine. Add the Parmigiano, garlic, eggs, and mozzarella, beating well to combine. Taste for seasonings.

3. Spray a large rimmed cookie sheet or jelly-roll pan with nonstick cooking spray. Turn the semolina mixture onto the cookie sheet, using a rubber spatula to scrape out the pot and to smooth the top. Bake for 35 minutes, or until the top is medium brown and crispy. Remove from the oven and use a large spoon to serve. Top each serving with a little of the heated marinara sauce.

Spinach Patties

SERVES 6

In my mother's house each dinner began with a new and exciting vegetable dish. Among my favorites were these little spinach patties, always delicious whether served hot or chilled. You can even take them along on a picnic.

2 (10-ounce) bags spinach, well washed and drained
Salt and pepper to taste
4 eggs
1/4 cup finely chopped flat-leaf parsley
1 small yellow onion, finely chopped
2 tablespoons unbleached all-purpose flour
1/4 cup grated Asiago cheese
2 cups plain dry bread crumbs
1/4 cup olive oil

1. Place the spinach with the water clinging to its leaves in a pot and add the salt and pepper. Cover and cook on medium heat, stirring occasionally, for 10 to 12 minutes, or until the spinach is wilted. Drain.

2. Coarsely chop the spinach and place it in a bowl. Add the eggs, parsley, onion, flour, cheese, and 1 cup of the bread crumbs and mix well. Taste for seasonings.

3. Spread the remaining cup of bread crumbs in a pie pan. Using about 1/4 cup per patty, form the spinach mixture into little patties. Dip each patty into the bread crumbs, turning to coat both sides.

4. Heat 2 tablespoons of the oil in a large nonstick skillet over medium heat. Place as many patties in the skillet as will fit without crowding. Cook for 2 to 3 minutes, or until medium brown, then turn and cook the other side for 2 to 3 minutes, or until medium brown. Transfer to a platter. Cook the remaining patties, heating additional oil as needed.

Cornmeal Loaves with Raisins and Fennel Seeds

SERVES 6

On February 3 we celebrate the feast of St. Blaise by going to church to have our throats blessed and then coming home to this dish. My mom's childhood friend Teresa Amendola continues the delicious tradition by sharing her cornmeal loaves with my mom each year and by sharing her recipe with me. This dish makes a filling dinner when served with Sautéed Spinach (page 54) and your favorite pasta tossed with marinara sauce.

7 **cups water**
1/2 **cup golden raisins**
1 **tablespoon fennel seeds**
3 **cups cornmeal**
   Salt and pepper to taste
1 **tablespoon olive oil**

1. Bring the water, raisins, and fennel seeds to a boil in a large covered pot over high heat. Put on a pair of oven mitts to protect your hands as you add the cornmeal because the mixture tends to bubble up like a volcano. Gradually pour in the cornmeal, whisking continuously as you pour. Lower the heat to medium. Whisk in the salt and pepper. Cook for 5 minutes, whisking frequently.

2. Spray a large rimmed cookie sheet or jelly-roll pan with nonstick cooking spray. Turn the cornmeal mixture onto the cookie sheet. Set aside until cool enough to handle.

3. Preheat the oven to 375 degrees. Spray another cookie sheet with nonstick cooking spray. Rub the olive oil onto the palms of your hands. Using your hands, form 1/2 cupfuls of the mixture into loaves. Arrange on the second cookie sheet, leaving 1 inch of space between them. Bake for 55 minutes, or until the loaves are golden brown and crisp to the touch.

Pizza Amalfitan Style

SERVES 6

This is a simple but delicious pizza made with canned tomatoes and lots of onions and topped with Parmesan cheese.

1 tablespoon unbleached all-purpose flour
1 pound pizza dough, thawed if frozen
3 tablespoons extra virgin olive oil
2 tablespoons cornmeal
1 (28-ounce) can Italian whole peeled tomatoes in juice, squeezed with your hands to crush
2 large cloves garlic, finely chopped
2 medium sweet onions, cut into thin slices
1 teaspoon dried oregano
Salt and pepper to taste
3 tablespoons grated Parmigiano-Reggiano cheese

1. Center the oven rack. Preheat the oven to 450 degrees. Spread the flour in a rectangle about 15 × 10 inches on your countertop. Place the pizza dough on the flour, then turn it to coat on all sides. Pat the dough with your fingertips for a few minutes to make it more pliable. Use a little of the flour on the counter to dust a rolling pin. Roll the dough into a 15 × 10-inch rectangle.

2. Brush a large cookie sheet with 1 tablespoon of the olive oil. Sprinkle the cornmeal evenly over the cookie sheet. Carefully transfer the pizza dough to the cookie sheet and reshape it if necessary with your fingertips.

3. Place the tomatoes, remaining 2 tablespoons of olive oil, the garlic, onions, oregano, salt, and pepper in a bowl and stir to mix. Spoon this mixture evenly over the pizza dough. Sprinkle the Parmigiano cheese evenly over the pizza. Bake for about 20 minutes, or until the underside of the crust is golden brown. Remove from the oven and carefully cut into 6 pieces.

Pizza Fritti

SERVES 6

Pizza fritti, *or "fried pizza," is something that we all have enjoyed at outdoor fairs across the country. When I was a little girl, my mom made big pots of pizza dough every Sunday during the fall and winter months, when the weather was cool. She made Pizza Amalfitan Style (page 166), Pizza Fritti, and Pizza Fritti Stuffed with Escarole and "Pepperoni" (page 170). Frying the pizza dough gives it the characteristic taste and crispy texture that no other method can match. Today we continue to enjoy these treats, but now we buy the pizza dough at a local pizza parlor or the supermarket. I like to keep several 1-pound bags of pizza dough in my freezer for convenience.*

    2 to 3 tablespoons unbleached all-purpose flour
    1 pound pizza dough, thawed if frozen
    1 cup canola oil
    1 cup Basil-Scented Marinara Sauce (page 150), heated
    3 tablespoons grated Parmigiano-Reggiano cheese

1. Scatter the flour on a countertop. Place the pizza dough on the flour and turn to coat on all sides. Cut the dough into 6 pieces. Roll each into a ball. One at a time, roll the dough into 8-inch rounds. Line a cookie sheet with a double layer of paper towels and set it by the stove.

2. Heat the oil in a large, deep skillet over medium heat. One at a time, fry the rounds of pizza dough for 2 to 3 minutes, or until they are medium golden brown on the undersides. Carefully turn the dough over, and fry the other sides for 2 to 3 minutes, or until medium golden brown. Transfer the fried rounds to the towel-lined cookie sheet.

3. To serve, place a fried round on a plate, spoon about 1/4 cup of heated marinara sauce over the top, then sprinkle with a little grated cheese.

Potato and Sausage Pizza

SERVES 4 TO 6

Little restaurants throughout southern Italy feature big sheet pans of beautiful pizzas in their windows. The following dish is a vegetarian variation on the delicious combination of sliced potatoes, fennel-scented sausages, and caramelized onion rings.

Note: Lightlife brand makes Lean Italian Links, available in health foods stores. Partially freeze the links for ease in cutting.

        4 **large boiling potatoes**
      1/4 **cup extra virgin olive oil, divided**
        1 **large yellow onion, cut into thin slices and separated into rings**
        1 **(12-ounce) package Italian-style meatless sausage links, cut into**
           small pieces
           Salt and pepper to taste
        2 **tablespoons unbleached all-purpose flour**
        1 **pound pizza dough, thawed if frozen**
        2 **tablespoons cornmeal**
      1/4 **cup grated Asiago cheese**
        4 **ounces mozzarella cheese, shredded**

1. Bring a large pot of lightly salted water to a boil over high heat. Add the potatoes, cover, and cook for 15 to 18 minutes, or until fork-tender. Drain. When cool enough to handle, peel off the skin. Cut into 1/3-inch-thick rounds.

2. Meanwhile, heat 3 tablespoons of the olive oil in a large skillet over medium heat. Add the onion, sausages, salt, and pepper. Cover and cook, stirring occasionally, for 15 minutes, or until the onion is golden brown but not burned.

3. Spread the flour evenly in about a 20-inch square on the countertop. Preheat the oven to 450 degrees. Place the dough on the flour and pat it with your fingertips to coat with flour, then turn and coat the other side. Roll the dough into a 20 × 16-inch rectangle.

4. Spray a large cookie sheet with nonstick cooking spray. Scatter the cornmeal evenly over the cookie sheet. Carefully transfer the pizza dough to the cookie sheet and reshape it if necessary with your fingertips. Arrange the potato slices evenly over the dough. Drizzle the remaining tablespoon of oil evenly over the potatoes. Sprinkle with salt and pepper. Scatter the onions and sausages evenly over the potatoes. Sprinkle the cheeses evenly on top. Bake for about 30 minutes, or until the underside of the crust is golden brown.

Pizza Fritti Stuffed with Escarole and "Pepperoni"

SERVES 6

My mom used to stuff her pizza dough with just about any leftover she had in the refrigerator, anything from sautéed escarole to peas and onions. I've never tasted one I didn't like.

Note: Meatless pepperoni is available in most health foods stores; a company named Yves makes this and other meatless, soy versions of familiar meats.

> 3 tablespoons extra virgin olive oil
> 3 large cloves garlic, finely chopped
> 2 large heads escarole, well washed and cut into 2-inch pieces
> Salt and pepper to taste
> 1 (4-ounce) package meatless pepperoni
> 2 tablespoons unbleached all-purpose flour
> 1 pound pizza dough, thawed if frozen
> 4 ounces mozzarella cheese, shredded
> 1 cup canola oil

1. Heat the olive oil in a large pot over medium heat. Add the garlic, escarole, salt, and pepper. Cover and cook, stirring occasionally, for about 10 minutes, or until the escarole is just tender. Stir in the pepperoni slices, mixing to combine. Taste for seasonings. Drain the mixture, then turn into a bowl.

2. Dust the countertop and a cookie sheet with the flour. Place the pizza dough on the floured counter and turn to coat evenly. Cut the dough into 6 equal pieces. Roll each into a ball. Roll each ball out into an 8-inch round.

3. Divide the escarole into 6 portions and place on one side of each dough round. Sprinkle the mozzarella evenly over the escarole. Fold the pizza dough over the filling and pinch the edges to seal. Transfer the stuffed pizza to the flour-dusted cookie sheet. Continue stuffing the remaining pizzas.

4. Place a double layer of paper towels on a cookie sheet and set it by the stove. Heat the canola oil in a large, deep skillet over medium heat. Arrange as many stuffed pizzas in the skillet as you can without crowding. Fry for 5 to 7 minutes, or until the undersides are medium golden brown. Turn and cook the other sides for 4 to 5 minutes, or until golden brown. Transfer to the towel-lined cookie sheet. Continue frying the remaining pizzas. Serve hot or at room temperature.

Tomato Bread

SERVES 6

Tomato bread comes out at its best toward the end of the summer, when tomatoes are at their most flavorful.

1 **tablespoon unbleached all-purpose flour**
1 **to 1¹/₄ pounds pizza dough, thawed if frozen**
2 **tablespoons extra virgin olive oil**
3 **large cloves garlic, finely chopped**
1 **medium sweet onion, finely chopped**
5 **ripe large tomatoes, cut into 1-inch cubes**
5 **large fresh basil leaves**
¹/₄ **cup finely chopped flat-leaf parsley**
Salt and pepper to taste
2 **tablespoons cornmeal**

1. Scatter the flour in a 16-inch square on the countertop. Place the pizza dough on the flour and turn to coat on all sides with the flour.

2. Heat the oil in a large skillet over medium heat. Add the garlic, onion, tomatoes, basil, parsley, salt, and pepper. Cook, stirring occasionally, for 10 minutes, or until the tomatoes are soft and have released their juices. Drain the tomato mixture in a colander set over a bowl. Save the juices to add to a soup or other dish.

3. Preheat the oven to 375 degrees. Spray a cookie sheet with nonstick cooking spray. Scatter the cornmeal evenly over the cookie sheet. Roll the pizza dough into a 14-inch square. Using a slotted spoon, spread the tomato mixture evenly down the center of the pizza dough in an 11 × 6-inch area. Lift one side of the dough over the filling to fully encase it. Gently press down on the edge to seal. Lift the other side of the dough over the top. Press to seal the edges.

4. Carefully turn the bread over so that you have the double layer of dough on the bottom (this will prevent the dough from getting soggy). Carefully transfer the bread to the prepared cookie sheet. Cut two or three 1-inch slits in the top of the dough. Bake the bread for about 40 minutes, or until the top and underside are golden brown. Serve hot or chilled.

Fresh Mozzarella in Bread

SERVES 4

This old Italian favorite is known as mozzarella en carrozza (*mozzarella in carriage*), *which I learned to cook from my longtime friend Mary Moniello. She serves it for dinner with a dish of sautéed greens, maybe broccoli rabe or escarole, and a fresh tomato salad. Fresh mozzarella (in Italian,* fiore di latte, *or "flower of the milk") is available in most supermarkets.*

12 ounces fresh mozzarella cheese
8 ($1/2$-inch-thick) slices soft-crusted Italian bread
4 eggs
2 tablespoons finely chopped flat-leaf parsley
Salt and pepper to taste
$1^1/_2$ cups plain dry bread crumbs
$1/_4$ cup olive oil
1 cup Basil-Scented Marinara Sauce (page 150), heated (optional)

1. Drain the mozzarella thoroughly. Cut the mozzarella into $3/_4$-inch-thick slices, then trim the slices to fit the slices of bread. Break the eggs into a shallow bowl. Add the parsley, salt, and pepper and beat with a fork to blend.

2. Measure the bread crumbs into a shallow bowl. Arrange 4 slices of bread on a cookie sheet. Place a slice of mozzarella cheese on each slice of bread. Cover with the other slices of bread. Press down with your hands to seal the edges all around and encase the mozzarella. Dip each sandwich into the beaten eggs, turning to coat evenly. Gently shake off the excess. Then dip each sandwich in the bread crumbs, turning to coat evenly. Gently shake off the excess. Return the coated sandwiches to the cookie sheet.

3. Set a platter by the stove. Heat 2 tablespoons of the oil in a large skillet over medium heat. Arrange as many sandwiches as will fit in the skillet without crowding. Cover and cook for 1 to 2 minutes, or until the underside is medium brown. Carefully turn the sandwiches over and cook, covered, on the other side for 1 to 2 minutes, or until medium brown. Transfer to a platter. Heat the remaining 2 tablespoons oil and cook the remaining sandwiches. Serve with warmed marinara sauce, if desired.

Fried Mozzarella Cheese

SERVES 4

At Claire's we usually serve this popular dish with warmed marinara sauce, a tossed salad, and fresh bread. At home I serve it with sautéed greens, usually escarole or broccoli rabe.

Note: Buy fresh mozzarella (usually packed in water) if it is available in your supermarket. The flavor is so much better.

> 1 pound mozzarella cheese, cut into 1/4-inch-thick slices
> 1/2 cup unbleached all-purpose flour
> Salt and pepper to taste
> 2 eggs
> 1/4 cup finely chopped flat-leaf parsley
> 1 cup plain dry bread crumbs
> 1/4 cup olive oil
> 2 cups Basil-Scented Marinara Sauce (page 150) (optional)

1. Place the slices of mozzarella cheese on a plate. Measure the flour into a shallow bowl. Season with salt and pepper. Break the eggs into a shallow bowl. Beat the eggs lightly with a fork. Add the parsley, salt, and pepper. Measure the bread crumbs into another shallow bowl.

2. Have 2 cookie sheets or platters handy. Line one with a double layer of paper towels and set it by the stove. Dredge a slice of mozzarella in the flour. Shake off the excess. Dip it in the eggs, turning to coat. Shake off excess. Dip each mozzarella slice into the bread crumbs, turning to coat completely, and place on the bare cookie sheet.

3. Heat 2 tablespoons of the oil in a large nonstick skillet over medium-high heat. Arrange as many slices in the skillet as you can fit in a single layer without crowding. Cook for about 1 minute, or until medium brown and just beginning to ooze. Carefully turn and cook the other side for about 1 minute, or until golden brown. Transfer the browned mozzarella slices to the towel-lined cookie sheet. Heat the remaining oil and cook the remaining slices. Serve with warmed marinara sauce, if desired.

Swiss Chard Calzone

SERVES 4

Calzone (calzoni *means "trousers" in Italian) are turnovers made with pizza dough and a filling. They allow for tremendous creativity. You can make them small for individual servings or large for cutting into serving pieces, and you can fill them with just about any combination that you like. Swiss chard is a cruciferous vegetable and a member of the beet family. You can use the giant green (or red) leaves and pale green stems as you would spinach. Like spinach, chard is a rich source of vitamins A and C and iron.*

    1   bunch green Swiss chard
    3   tablespoons extra virgin olive oil
    1   small yellow onion, finely chopped
    2   large cloves garlic, coarsely chopped
        Salt and pepper to taste
    1   pound ricotta cheese
    2   eggs
    4   large fresh basil leaves, coarsely chopped
  1/4   cup grated Parmigiano-Reggiano cheese
    2   tablespoons unbleached all-purpose flour
    1   pound pizza dough, thawed if frozen
    2   tablespoons coarse cornmeal

1. Cut off and discard the bottom 6 inches of tough stems from the chard. Thoroughly wash the chard in plenty of water, lifting the leaves out to rinse away the grit. Drain the chard. Separate the leaves from the stems. Coarsely chop the leaves and thinly slice the stems; place in separate bowls.

2. Heat the oil in a large skillet over medium heat. Add the onion, garlic, chard stems, salt, and pepper. Stir to coat the vegetables with oil. Cover and cook for 5 minutes, stirring occasionally. Add the chard leaves, cover, and continue to cook, stirring occasionally, for 7 to 8 minutes, or until the stems and leaves are tender. Drain the mixture in a colander.

3. Turn the chard mixture into a bowl. Add the ricotta, eggs, basil, and Parmigiano cheese. Stir well to combine. Taste for seasonings.

4. Preheat the oven to 375 degrees. Spray a cookie sheet with nonstick cooking spray. Scatter the cornmeal evenly over the cookie sheet. Scatter the flour over a large area of countertop. Place the pizza dough on the flour and turn to coat on all sides. Using a rolling pin, roll the dough into an 18-inch square. Spoon the filling onto the right half of the pizza dough, leaving a 1-inch border around the edges. Lift the left half of the pizza dough over the filling. Press the edges to seal the dough. Carefully transfer the calzone to the prepared pan. Using a sharp knife, cut three 1-inch slits on the top of the calzone to allow steam to escape. Bake the calzone for 55 to 60 minutes, or until golden brown.

Spinach Risotto

SERVES 6

Risotto dishes are usually made with Arborio, a rice that has long and plump grains that are like little sponges that fill up with all the delicious flavors you can add. In order to get the creamy consistency of this dish, you must give it your full attention, stirring it for about 20 minutes, but the results will be worth it.

   5 **cups water**
   1 **(10-ounce) bag spinach, washed, tough stems removed, finely chopped**
      Salt and pepper to taste
   3 **tablespoons extra virgin olive oil**
   1 **large red Bermuda onion, finely chopped**
$2^1/_2$ **cups Arborio rice**
   1 **small zucchini, cut into tiny pieces**
   2 **ounces grated pecorino Romano cheese**

1. Measure the water into a large pot. Add the spinach, salt, and pepper, cover, and bring to a boil over high heat. Immediately turn off the heat and keep the spinach broth covered on the stove.

2. Heat the oil in a large skillet over medium-low heat. Add the onion. Sprinkle with salt and pepper. Cook, stirring occasionally, for 5 minutes, or until the onion is softened. Add the rice and zucchini. Cook for 5 minutes, stirring frequently. Add 1 cup of the spinach broth. Stir well to combine. Cook, stirring constantly, for about 2 minutes, or until the rice absorbs the broth.

3. Add another $^1/_2$ cup of spinach broth. Cook, stirring constantly, for about 2 minutes, or until the rice absorbs the broth. Continue adding the remaining spinach broth $^1/_2$ cup at a time, stirring continuously for 2 minutes after each addition, or until the broth is absorbed into the rice. Taste the rice for doneness. The risotto should be barely tender, thick, and creamy when it is done. Stir in the cheese. Taste for seasonings.

Risotto with Smoked Mozzarella and Green Peas

SERVES 6

This dish was inspired by the risottos that I have enjoyed in Baci, a lovely Italian restaurant in Boca Raton, Florida.

>   5 cups water
>   2 medium carrots, peeled and diced
>   1 medium parsnip, peeled and diced
>   1 bay leaf
>   1 teaspoon dried sage
>   Salt and pepper to taste
>   3 tablespoons extra virgin olive oil
>   1 medium red onion, finely chopped
> 2¹/₂ cups Arborio rice (Italian risotto rice)
>   2 cups frozen tiny green peas, thawed
>   8 ounces smoked mozzarella cheese, cut into small cubes

1. Combine the water, carrots, parsnip, bay leaf, sage, salt, and pepper in a large pot. Cover and bring to a boil over high heat, then lower the heat to medium-low and cook at a medium boil, stirring occasionally, for about 15 minutes, or until the parsnip is tender. Drain in a colander set over a bowl. Reserve the broth and vegetables separately.

2. Heat the oil in a large skillet over medium-low heat. Add the onion and sprinkle with salt and pepper. Cook, stirring occasionally, for 5 minutes, or until the onion is softened. Add the rice, stirring to coat with the oil. Cook for 5 minutes, stirring frequently.

3. Add 1 cup of the reserved broth. Stir constantly for about 2 minutes, or until the rice absorbs the broth. Add the remaining broth ¹/₂ cup at a time, stirring continuously for about 2 minutes after each addition, or until the broth is absorbed by the rice. Taste the rice for doneness. Remove from the heat.

4. Stir in the reserved vegetables, the green peas, and the smoked mozzarella, stirring until the cheese melts slightly and the risotto is thick and creamy. Taste for seasonings. Serve immediately.

Artichoke Hearts in Marinara Sauce with Rice and Peas

SERVES 6

This is a rich stewlike dish from Sorrento, best when served with plenty of crusty Italian bread for sopping up the sauce.

- 1/4 cup extra virgin olive oil
- 1 medium yellow onion, finely chopped
- 3 large cloves garlic, coarsely chopped
- 1/2 teaspoon red pepper flakes
- 1/2 cup finely chopped flat-leaf parsley
- 1 (28-ounce) can Italian tomato puree
- 4 cups water
- 1 large bay leaf
- 10 large fresh basil leaves
  Salt and pepper to taste
- 1 cup Arborio rice (Italian risotto rice)
- 1 (14-ounce) can artichoke hearts, drained and cut into thin slices
- 2 cups frozen tiny green peas, thawed

1. Heat the oil in a large pot over medium-low heat. Add the onion, garlic, red pepper flakes, and parsley. Cover and cook, stirring occasionally, for about 5 minutes, or until the onion is softened.

2. Add the tomato puree, water, bay leaf, basil, salt, and pepper. Raise the heat to medium, cover, and cook at a medium boil for 25 minutes, stirring occasionally.

3. Stir in the rice. Cover and continue to cook, stirring frequently to prevent sticking, for 20 minutes, or until the rice is tender.

4. Add the artichoke hearts and peas. Stir well to combine. Continue to cook for 3 to 4 minutes, stirring occasionally. Taste for seasonings.

Stewed Zucchini and Tomatoes over Arborio Rice

SERVES 6

This lovely stew tastes best when made during the summer, when zucchini and tomatoes are garden fresh.

- 3 tablespoons extra virgin olive oil
- 1 large yellow onion, cut into thick ribs
- 4 medium zucchini (about 1³/₄ pounds), cut into 1-inch-thick slices
- 2 large cloves garlic, coarsely chopped
- 3 ripe large tomatoes, cut into 1-inch-thick wedges
- 1 teaspoon dried oregano
  Salt and pepper to taste
- ¹/₄ cup dry white wine
- 4 cups cooked Arborio rice (Italian risotto rice)

1. Heat the oil in a large pot over medium-low heat. Add the onion, zucchini, garlic, tomatoes, oregano, salt, and pepper. Stir to coat the vegetables with oil. Cover and cook, stirring occasionally, for about 25 minutes, or until the vegetables are just tender.

2. Add the wine. Cover and continue to cook, stirring occasionally, for 5 minutes, or until the zucchini is tender. Taste for seasonings. Spread the cooked rice in a serving dish. Spoon the vegetables and their juices evenly over the rice.

Stuffed Zucchini

SERVES 6

My non-Italian friends are both amazed and delighted by the number of vegetables that we Italians tend to stuff. We do love our stuffed peppers and mushrooms and toma-toes, onions, escarole, cabbage, potatoes, artichokes, eggplant . . . and zucchini.

6 medium zucchini (7 to 8 inches long)
6 (1-inch-thick) slices hard Italian bread
4 large cloves garlic, coarsely chopped
3 tablespoons finely chopped flat-leaf parsley
2 medium mushrooms, finely chopped
1 small onion, finely chopped
1 ripe small tomato, finely chopped, including juices
2 tablespoons extra virgin olive oil
1 egg
2 tablespoons coarsely chopped fresh mint or 2 teaspoons dried
2 tablespoons grated Parmigiano-Reggiano cheese
Salt and pepper to taste

1. Cut a thin lengthwise slice from each zucchini so that it will lie flat in a baking pan. Then create a cavity down the center of each zucchini about 5 inches long, $1^1/_2$ inches wide, and 1 inch deep. Sprinkle the zucchini with salt.

2. Place the slices of bread in a bowl. Cover with hot tap water. Let the bread absorb the water for about 10 minutes. Turn the bread into a colander and press out as much water as you can. You should have about 2 cups of bread. Place the bread in a large bowl.

3. Preheat the oven to 400 degrees. Add the remaining ingredients to the drained bread. Mix well and taste for seasonings.

4. Spray a 13 × 9-inch baking pan with nonstick cooking spray. Fill the zuc-chini cavities with the stuffing. Arrange the zucchini in a single layer in the prepared baking dish. Pour $1^1/_2$ cups of water around, not over, the zucchini. Bake, uncov-ered, on the lower rack of the oven for about 1 hour, or until the zucchini are tender when tested with a fork and the stuffing is light to medium brown.

Stuffed Fryers

SERVES 6

My mom always referred to the long, pale green peppers as fryers because she fried them. In the supermarket these mild peppers are called Cubanelles. They are delicious fried or sautéed, especially if you first stuff them with a simple traditional Italian bread crumb stuffing, as in this recipe.

> 6 **large Cubanelle peppers**
> 2 **cups plain dry bread crumbs**
> 1/2 **cup coarsely chopped flat-leaf parsley**
> 1/4 **cup grated Asiago cheese**
> 1/4 **cup large green Italian olives, pitted and coarsely chopped**
> 3 **tablespoons extra virgin olive oil**
>   **Salt and pepper to taste**
> 1/4 **cup olive oil**

1. Rinse the peppers, cut off the tops, and remove the seeds and ribs from inside the peppers. Rinse and drain.

2. Place the bread crumbs, parsley, cheese, and olives in a bowl and toss to mix. Drizzle the extra virgin olive oil evenly over the top. Sprinkle lightly with salt (the cheese and the olives are salty) and pepper. Toss well to combine. Taste for seasonings. Stuff this mixture into the peppers, packing tightly.

3. Heat the 1/4 cup of olive oil in a large skillet over medium heat. Place the peppers on their sides in a single layer in the skillet. Cover and cook for 5 minutes, or until medium golden brown but not burned. Using tongs, turn the peppers over. Cover and cook for about 3 to 4 minutes, or until the undersides are medium golden brown.

Red Bell Peppers Stuffed with Arborio Rice and Artichoke Hearts

SERVES 6

There are many vegetarian stuffings that go well with sweet red peppers, and this is one of my favorites.

4 **large red bell peppers, cut in half and seeded**
   Salt and pepper to taste
3 **tablespoons extra virgin olive oil**
1 **medium yellow onion, finely chopped**
2 **ribs celery, finely chopped**
3 **cups cooked Arborio rice (Italian risotto rice)**
1 **(14-ounce) can artichoke hearts, drained and coarsely chopped**
1 **plum tomato, finely chopped, including juices**
1/4 **cups coarsely chopped fresh mint or 1 tablespoon dried**
2 **tablespoons finely chopped flat-leaf parsley**
2 **tablespoon capers, drained**
3 **tablespoons fresh lemon juice (about 1 lemon)**

1. Sprinkle the peppers with salt and pepper. Preheat the oven to 400 degrees.

2. Heat the oil in a large nonstick skillet over medium heat. Add the onion, celery, salt, and pepper. Cover and cook, stirring occasionally, for about 4 minutes, or until the onion is softened. Turn the mixture into a bowl, using a rubber spatula to scrape out the skillet.

3. Add the cooked rice, artichoke hearts, tomato, mint, parsley, capers, lemon juice, salt, and pepper. Stir to mix well. Taste for seasonings. Stuff this mixture into the pepper halves. Arrange the peppers in a glass baking dish large enough to hold them in one layer. Pour 1 cup of water around, not over, the peppers. Cover the pan tightly with foil. Bake for about 1 hour, or until the peppers are fork-tender.

Red Bell Peppers Stuffed with Mashed Potatoes

SERVES 6

Our dear family friend Duke Meoli inspired this creative alternative to the bread stuffing popular in many Italian homes. Serve it with White Bean and Mint Salad (page 96) and Sautéed Broccoli Rabe (page 39) for a memorable dinner.

6 medium baking potatoes, peeled and cut into eighths
2 tablespoons extra virgin olive oil
1 medium sweet onion, finely chopped
1 medium clove garlic, finely chopped
1 medium zucchini, diced
1/2 teaspoon dried oregano
Salt and pepper to taste
1/4 cup soy milk
1/4 cup freshly grated Parmigiano-Reggiano cheese
3 tablespoons coarsely chopped flat-leaf parsley
6 large red bell peppers, cut in half and seeded

1. Preheat the oven to 400 degrees. Place the potatoes in a large pot and add water to cover by 3 inches. Cover and bring to a boil over high heat. Lower the heat to medium and cook at a medium boil for about 12 minutes, or until the potatoes are fork-tender. Drain.

2. While the potatoes are cooking, heat the oil in a large skillet over medium heat. Add the onion, garlic, zucchini, oregano, salt, and pepper. Cover and cook, stirring frequently, for 3 minutes, or until the zucchini is softened.

3. After draining the potatoes, return them to the pot. Add the soy milk, salt, and pepper. Mash the potatoes but leave them a little lumpy. Add the sautéed vegetable mixture, using a rubber spatula to scrape out the skillet. Add the grated cheese and parsley. Stir to mix well. Taste for seasonings.

4. Fill the pepper halves with the mashed potato mixture, about 1/2 cup per half. Spray a large baking pan with olive oil cooking spray. Arrange the filled pepper halves in a single layer in the prepared pan. Add 1 cup of water to the pan around, not over, the peppers. Cover the pan tightly with foil. Bake for 45 to 60 minutes, or until the peppers are fork-tender. Remove the foil and continue baking for 15 minutes, or until the potatoes are golden brown.

Stuffed Onions

SERVES 6

We stuff huge, sweet onions with a mixture of bread and ground meatless beef, then bake them until golden. Serve them with mashed potatoes (pages 30, 32) and Sautéed Spinach (page 54) to complete the meal.

2 (1-inch-thick) slices Italian bread
1 (16-ounce) package meatless ground "beef"
2 tablespoons finely chopped flat-leaf parsley
1 large clove garlic, finely chopped
3 leaves fresh basil, finely chopped
1 rib celery, finely chopped
1 ripe small tomato, finely chopped
3 tablespoons extra virgin olive oil
1 egg
1/4 cup grated Asiago cheese
   Salt and pepper to taste
12 medium sweet onions, peeled

1. Place the bread in a shallow bowl. Cover with hot tap water. Set aside to absorb some of the water and to soften. After about 5 minutes, turn the bread into a colander and press out as much water as you can. Place the bread in a bowl. Add the ground "beef," parsley, garlic, basil, celery, tomato, oil, egg, cheese, salt, and pepper. Mix well to combine. Taste for seasonings.

2. Preheat the oven to 400 degrees. Carefully cut a hole large and deep enough to hold about 1/4 cup of filling into the stem end of each onion. Sprinkle the onions with salt and pepper. Stuff the onions with the bread mixture, mounding on top.

3. Spray a rectangular baking pan large enough to hold the onions with nonstick cooking spray. Arrange the stuffed onions in the pan. Pour 1 cup of water into the pan around, not over, the onions. Cover the pan with foil, tenting it to keep from crushing the filling. Bake for about 1 hour, until the onions are fork-tender.

Stuffed Portobello Mushrooms

SERVES 4

Prepare a filling of ground "beef," artichoke hearts, fresh garlic, and sun-dried tomatoes, then stuff meaty portobello mushroom caps, and you'll have a very special dinner entree. Serve them with Roasted-Garlic Mashed Potatoes (page 30), Porcini Mushroom Gravy (page 49), Sautéed Carrots with Onions and Green Peas (page 45), Zabaglione (page 231), and espresso for a memorable meal.

4 **large portobello mushroom caps (about 4 inches across)**
1 **(1-inch-thick) slice Italian bread**
14 **ounces meatless ground "beef," thawed if frozen**
2 **canned artichoke hearts, drained and coarsely chopped**
1 **sun-dried tomato in oil, drained and finely chopped**
2 **large cloves garlic, finely chopped**
1/2 **small onion, finely chopped**
1 **tablespoon finely chopped flat-leaf parsley**
1 **large fresh basil leaf, coarsely chopped**
1 **egg**
1 **tablespoon extra virgin olive oil**
  Salt and pepper to taste

1. Preheat the oven to 375 degrees. Rinse the mushroom caps and drain, stem side down, on paper towels. Place the bread in a bowl. Cover with hot tap water. Set aside until the bread has absorbed some of the water and is cool enough to handle. Turn the bread into a colander and press out as much water as possible. You should have about 1/3 cup of bread.

2. Place the "beef" in a bowl. Add the artichoke hearts, sun-dried tomato, garlic, onion, parsley, basil, egg, 2 teaspoons of the olive oil, the drained bread, and salt and pepper. Mix well to combine.

3. Spray a 13 × 9-inch baking pan with nonstick cooking spray. Brush the mushroom caps with the remaining teaspoon of olive oil. Sprinkle with salt and pepper. Stuff the filling into the mushroom caps. Arrange the stuffed mushrooms in a single layer in the baking pan. Pour 1/2 cup of water around, not over, the mushrooms. Bake for 55 to 60 minutes, or until the mushrooms are fork-tender and the filling is crispy on top.

Pan-Seared Herb-Crusted Portobello Mushrooms

SERVES 4 TO 6

My grandmother frequently breaded and pan-fried mushrooms and many other vegetables, and so did my mom. The wonderful flavor and the crispy texture of pan-fried foods cannot be duplicated without using olive oil, so I do occasionally indulge, particularly on Christmas Eve, when we traditionally serve a mixture of pan-fried foods. Serve these crunchy and delicious mushrooms on Christmas Eve or for a special dinner any time.

1 **cup unbleached all-purpose flour**
   Salt and pepper to taste
4 **eggs**
3 **tablespoons finely chopped fresh spearmint**
2 **tablespoons finely chopped flat-leaf parsley**
2 **large cloves garlic, minced**
2 **cups plain dry bread crumbs**
8 **large portobello mushroom caps (about 12 ounces), rinsed and drained**
6 **tablespoons olive oil**

1. Measure the flour into a shallow bowl. Season with salt and pepper. Stir to combine.

2. Break the eggs into a small bowl, then whisk lightly to blend. Add the spearmint, parsley, garlic, salt, and pepper. Whisk to mix.

3. Measure the bread crumbs into a shallow bowl. Have a cookie sheet close by to hold the mushrooms after you bread them and a platter set by the stove for the cooked mushroom caps.

4. Dredge a mushroom cap in the seasoned flour. Shake off the excess. Dip into the beaten eggs to coat. Hold the mushroom cap stem side up, allowing the shallow cavity to fill with the egg mixture. Lift the mushroom cap out of the egg mixture, keeping as much of the beaten eggs in the cavity as possible. Set the mushroom cap in the bread crumbs and cover it with the crumbs, pressing them into the cavity and coating the rounded side. Transfer the coated mushroom cap to the cookie sheet. Repeat with the remaining mushroom caps.

5. Heat 3 tablespoons of the olive oil in a large nonstick skillet over medium heat. Arrange as many of the coated mushrooms as will fit in the skillet in a single layer without crowding (4 should fit). Cover and cook for 4 to 5 minutes, or until the mushrooms are medium dark brown and crispy but not burned. Turn the mushroom caps, cover, and cook the other side for 3 to 4 minutes, or until they are medium dark brown and tender when a fork is inserted into the side. Transfer the cooked mushrooms to a platter. Heat the remaining 3 tablespoons of olive oil and cook the remaining mushrooms.

Portobello Mushrooms with Cannellini Beans

SERVES 6

Serves this flavorful, stewlike dish in a rimmed bowl with good Italian bread for sopping up the luscious juices.

> 3 tablespoons extra virgin olive oil
> 1 medium sweet onion, cut into $1/2$-inch-thick ribs
> 2 large cloves garlic, finely chopped
> 4 large portobello mushrooms, cut into $3/4$-inch-thick slices
>   Salt and pepper to taste
> 3 large, ripe tomatoes, cut into 1-inch-thick wedges
> $1/4$ cup port wine
> 1 tablespoon fresh rosemary leaves
> 1 (19-ounce) can cannellini beans, drained

1. Heat the oil in a large skillet over medium heat. Add the onion, garlic, mushrooms, salt, and pepper. Stir to combine. Cover and cook, stirring occasionally, for 5 to 7 minutes, or until the mushrooms release some of their liquid. Add the tomatoes, port, and rosemary leaves.

2. Raise the heat to medium-high, and continue cooking, covered, stirring occasionally, for about 5 minutes, or until the tomatoes are barely tender.

3. Stir in the cannellini beans, mixing well to combine. Continue cooking, uncovered, stirring occasionally, for about 5 minutes, or until the mixture has reduced slightly. Taste for seasonings.

Italian Hamburgers

SERVES 4

Italian hamburgers are prepared much like meatballs, with bread, parsley, and garlic. My mother always referred to regular hamburgers as blue plates, and that was something that she, like her mom, was not interested in cooking for her family. When they did cook with meats, the meats were always embellished with traditional ingredients, and these burgers are no exception. They make a delicious entree either pan-fried or baked, with or without a bun.

- 3 (1-inch-thick) slices hard Italian bread
- 1 (14-ounce) package meatless ground "beef," thawed if frozen
- 1/4 cup coarsely chopped flat-leaf parsley
- 1 egg
- 2 large cloves garlic, finely chopped
- 2 tablespoons olive oil
- Salt and pepper to taste

1. Place the bread in a bowl. Cover with hot tap water. Set aside for about 5 minutes to soften and absorb some of the water. Turn into a colander and press out as much water as you can. Turn into a bowl.

2. Add the ground "beef," parsley, egg, garlic, 1 tablespoon of the olive oil, and the salt and pepper. Using your hands, mix the ingredients until well combined. Form into 4 burgers.

3. Heat the remaining tablespoon of olive oil in a large skillet over medium-low heat. Arrange the burgers in a single layer in the heated oil. Cover and cook for about 8 minutes, or until the undersides are well browned but not burned. Turn the burgers, cover the skillet, and cook the other sides for about 5 minutes, or until the burgers are well browned but not burned.

Vegetarian Meat Loaf with Roasted White and Sweet Potatoes, Onions, and Carrots

SERVES 6 TO 8

The most enticing aroma will fill your kitchen as this one-pan meal bakes in the oven. And any leftover meat loaf makes a terrific sandwich on Italian bread with sliced tomato and onion and a little mayonnaise. You don't even need to reheat it.

Meat Loaf:
>   8 (1-inch-thick) slices Italian bread
>   1 (14-ounce) package meatless ground "beef," thawed if frozen
>   1/2 cup coarsely chopped flat-leaf parsley
>   2 large cloves garlic, finely chopped
>   1 small sweet onion, finely chopped
>   1 egg or 1/4 cup egg substitute
>   1 tablespoon extra virgin olive oil
>   Salt and pepper to taste

Roasted Vegetables:
>   6 medium baking potatoes, cut lengthwise into 6 wedges
>   2 large sweet potatoes, cut lengthwise into 6 wedges
>   2 large carrots, peeled and cut into 1/2-inch-thick slices
>   2 medium sweet onions, cut in half, then into thick ribs
>   3 large cloves garlic, coarsely chopped
>   1 tablespoon extra virgin olive oil
>   Salt and pepper to taste
>   1 cup Basil-Scented Marinara Sauce (page 150) (optional)

1. Center the oven rack. Preheat the oven to 375 degrees. Spray a large roasting pan with nonstick cooking spray.

2. To make the meat loaf, place the bread in a bowl. Cover with hot tap water. Set aside to soften for about 5 minutes. Turn into a colander and press out as much water as you can. Turn the drained bread into a large bowl. Add the ground "beef," parsley, garlic, onion, egg, and oil. Sprinkle with salt and pepper. Mix well with your hands to combine. Taste for seasonings.

3. Place the meat mixture in the center of the prepared baking pan. Using your hands, form it into a loaf about 8 × 5 inches. Pat the loaf smooth.

4. To prepare the vegetables, place the potatoes, carrots, onions, and garlic in a large bowl. Toss well to mix. Drizzle with the olive oil, sprinkle with salt and pepper, and toss well to combine.

5. Arrange the vegetable mixture in the pan around the meat loaf. Pour the marinara sauce over the meat loaf if you are using it. Cover the pan tightly with foil. Bake for 40 minutes, then remove the foil and continue baking for 35 minutes, or until the potatoes are fork-tender.

Green Bean, Tomato, Potato, and Meatball Stew

SERVES 6

This is the perfect stew for a cold winter night. All you need to add is some crusty Italian bread for a wonderful supper.

Note: I used Gimme Lean "Beef," available in health foods stores, for this recipe, although there are other brands, such as Morningstar Farms and Pillsbury.

 2 (1-inch-thick) slices hard Italian bread
 1 (14-ounce) package ground "beef"
 1/2 cup finely chopped flat-leaf parsley
 4 large cloves garlic, finely chopped
 1 egg
 5 tablespoons extra virgin olive oil
 Salt and pepper to taste
 1 medium yellow onion, cut into thick ribs
 3/4 pound green beans, trimmed and cut into 1-inch pieces
 3 large potatoes, peeled and cut into 2-inch pieces
 2 (28-ounce) cans Italian whole peeled tomatoes, squeezed with
 your hands to crush
 1/2 cup water
 10 large fresh basil leaves
 2 bay leaves
 1 teaspoon dried oregano

1. Place the bread in a bowl and cover with hot tap water. Set aside for 5 to 10 minutes, or until cool enough to handle. Drain the bread in a colander and press out as much of the water as possible. Turn into a large bowl.

2. Add the ground "beef," 1/4 cup of the chopped parsley, 1 clove of the chopped garlic, the egg, 1 teaspoon of the olive oil, and salt and pepper. Mix well with your hands or a spoon.

3. Roll heaping tablespoons of the mixture into about 16 balls. Set aside on a platter or cookie sheet. Heat the remaining olive oil in a large pot over medium heat. Add the remaining chopped garlic, the onion, green beans, potatoes, remaining chopped parsley, and salt and pepper. Cover and cook, stirring occasionally, for 15 minutes, or until the vegetables have released some of their juices.

4. Add the tomatoes and their juices, the water, basil, bay leaves, and oregano. Stir well to mix. Cover and cook at a medium boil (it will reach a boil after about 5 minutes) for about 40 minutes, stirring occasionally.

5. Meanwhile, spray a large nonstick skillet with olive oil cooking spray. Heat the skillet over medium-high heat. Arrange the "meatballs" in the heated skillet without crowding them too much. Brown each side for about 2 minutes, then transfer them to the cookie sheet. Carefully lower the "meatballs" into the sauce, using a wooden spoon to gently push them into the sauce to cover. Cover and cook for 20 minutes without stirring, then stir gently to mix, trying not to break up the "meatballs." Taste for seasonings.

Meatless Italian Sausages Roasted with Mushrooms, Onions, Potatoes, and Peas

SERVES 4

The aroma of fennel-scented Italian sausages roasting with vegetables will fill your kitchen and welcome all who enter. And wait until you taste this combination. Simply add some good, crusty Italian bread, a glass of a beautiful Chianti for the adults, and grape juice mixed with Italian sparkling water for the children, and you will have a lovely meal that is especially nice during the winter months.

Note: I used Lightlife brand Lean Links Italian sausages, available in health foods stores and in many supermarkets.

- 3 **large potatoes, peeled and cut into spears**
- 2 **medium onions, cut into thick ribs**
- 2 **carrots, peeled and cut diagonally into $1/2$-inch-thick slices**
- 2 **large portobello mushroom caps, quartered**
- 1 **(11-ounce) package meatless Italian sausages, quartered**
- 3 **tablespoons extra virgin olive oil**
- 3 **tablespoons balsamic vinegar**
- 1 **tablespoon fennel seeds**
  Salt and pepper to taste
- 2 **cups frozen green peas**

1. Preheat the oven to 400 degrees. Place the potatoes, onions, carrots, mushroom caps, and sausages in a bowl. Toss gently to mix. Drizzle the olive oil and vinegar evenly over the mixture. Scatter the fennel seeds, salt, and pepper on top. Toss well to mix.

2. Spray a roasting pan with olive oil cooking spray. Turn the mixture into the prepared pan, using a rubber spatula to scrape the bowl of any juices and to spread the mixture evenly in the pan. Bake, stirring occasionally, for about $1^3/4$ hours, or until the potatoes are fork-tender. Stir in the green peas. Continue cooking for 5 minutes.

Sausage and Pepper Rolls

SERVES 6

Visit any Italian festival and you will smell the wonderful aroma of sausage and peppers, grilling with onions. Enjoy that same terrific pleasure with this delicious and healthy recipe.

2 tablespoons unbleached all-purpose flour
1 pound pizza dough, thawed if frozen
2 tablespoons extra virgin olive oil
3 medium sweet onions, cut in half, then into thick ribs
2 cloves garlic, finely chopped
5 medium red bell peppers, cut in half, seeded, and sliced into $1/2$-inch ribs
$1/2$ teaspoon dried oregano
1 teaspoon fennel seeds
$1/4$ teaspoon red pepper flakes
Salt and pepper to taste
6 links meatless sausages, thawed, cut in half lengthwise

1. Spread the flour in a 12-inch circle on the countertop. Place the dough on the flour and gently pat it to coat with the flour, then turn the dough over and coat the other side with flour. Set aside while you prepare the filling.

2. Preheat the oven to 400 degrees. Heat the olive oil in a large nonstick skillet over medium-high heat. Add the onions, garlic, and peppers. Scatter the oregano, fennel seeds, crushed red pepper flakes, salt, and pepper evenly over the vegetables. Cover and cook for 5 minutes, then stir to mix. Cover and continue to cook, stirring occasionally, for 6 to 8 minutes, or until the peppers and onions are just tender. Lower the heat to medium if they begin to burn. Taste for seasonings. Remove from the heat and set aside.

3. Heat a large nonstick skillet over medium-high heat. Spray the skillet with olive oil cooking spray. Arrange the meatless sausages, cut side down, in a single layer in the skillet. Cook for 2 to 3 minutes, or until golden brown, then carefully turn the sausages and lightly brown the other sides. Set aside.

4. Spray 2 cookie sheets with olive oil cooking spray. Cut the pizza dough into 6 equal pieces. Using a rolling pin, begin rolling one piece of dough into an

8 × 8-inch square. Sprinkle lightly with flour if the dough gets sticky. Using tongs, arrange about one-sixth of the peppers and onions in a row down the center of the dough. Arrange 2 pieces of the sausage over the vegetables. Encase the mixture by gently bringing one side of the dough over the filling and pressing gently to seal. Then bring the other side of the dough over the filled dough to create a sausage and pepper roll. Pinch the edges and ends of the dough together to seal.

5. Transfer the roll to a prepared cookie sheet. Repeat the process until all 6 pieces of dough are filled. Leave 3 inches between the rolls for even baking. Bake for 10 minutes, then rotate the cookie sheets from top to bottom and continue baking for another 6 to 8 minutes, or until golden brown. Serve hot.

Sausage Pizzaiola Style

SERVES 4

This delicious meal is also convenient to make. Cook it in one pot on top of the stove, and in a short time you can enjoy a complete dinner—and have only one pot to wash!

1/4 **cup olive oil**
  2 **large yellow onions, cut into thick ribs**
  1 **(11-ounce) package meatless Italian sausages, cut into 1-inch-thick slices**
  1 **pound medium mushrooms, quartered**
    Salt and pepper to taste
  1 **(28-ounce) can crushed Italian tomatoes**
  2 **cups water**
  4 **medium potatoes, peeled and cut into 1-inch cubes**
  1 **tablespoon dried oregano**
1/4 **cup dry red wine**
1/4 **cup finely chopped flat-leaf parsley**
  1 **cup frozen green peas, thawed**

1. Heat the olive oil in a large sauce pot over medium heat. Add the onions, sausages, mushrooms, salt, and pepper. Cover and cook, stirring occasionally, for 15 minutes, or until the onions are soft.

2. Add the tomatoes, water, potatoes, oregano, wine, and parsley. Stir to combine. Cover and bring to a medium boil (this will take about 15 minutes). Cook at a medium boil, stirring occasionally, for about 30 minutes, or until the potatoes are tender.

3. Stir in the green peas. Cook, stirring occasionally, for 1 to 2 minutes, or until the peas are heated through. Taste for seasonings.

Pastina and Sausage Pie

SERVES 6

Pastina, the tiny bits of pasta, combined with meatless Italian-style sausages makes a delicious pie. You can enjoy it for a light lunch or with side dishes of Green Beans Stewed with Tomatoes (page 61), and Sautéed Endive (page 52) for a fine supper.

Note: I use Lightlife brand Lean Links Italian-style tofu sausages for this recipe. You can find them in health foods stores. Ronzoni is one of the few brands of pastina.

1¹/₃ cups pastina (tiny pasta bits)
  2 tablespoons olive oil
  1 large clove garlic, finely chopped
  1 small yellow onion, cut into thin slices and separated into rings
  2 medium zucchini (about ³/₄ pound), cut into ¹/₄-inch-thick rounds
 ¹/₂ (11-ounce) package meatless Italian-style sausages, finely chopped
    Salt and pepper to taste
  7 eggs, lightly beaten
  2 tablespoons minced flat-leaf parsley
 ¹/₄ cup grated Parmigiano-Reggiano cheese

1. Preheat the oven to 350 degrees. Cook and drain the pastina according to package directions.

2. Meanwhile, heat the olive oil in a large nonstick skillet over medium heat. Add the garlic, onion, zucchini, sausages, salt, and pepper. Cook, stirring occasionally, for 8 minutes, or until the zucchini is barely tender. Turn the mixture into a bowl, using a rubber spatula to scrape the skillet of the juices. Add the cooked pastina to the bowl, then the eggs, parsley, and cheese. Stir to combine.

3. Spray a 10-inch glass pie dish with olive oil cooking spray. Turn the mixture into the prepared dish, using a rubber spatula to scrape the bowl of its contents and to smooth the top. Bake for about 50 minutes, or until the top is golden brown and the center is set. Cut the pie into 6 wedges and serve either hot or chilled.

Broccoli Rabe and Sausage Pinwheel Bread

MAKES ABOUT 18 (1-INCH) SLICES FOR APPETIZERS, OR 4 ENTREE SERVINGS

Vegetable breads are an old Italian favorite. Although they are most often filled with broccoli or spinach, you can use tomatoes, eggplant, zucchini, or most other vegetables. At Claire's Corner Copia we serve them as an entree with warm marinara sauce on the side. And in my home there is usually a vegetable bread, cut into slices, that is served as an appetizer before dinner when my brothers and their families come. Any leftovers are wonderful for a picnic or for the next day's lunch.

Note: Vegetarian sausages, sometimes called tofu sausages or meatless sausages, can be found in the frozen foods section of most supermarkets.

> 1 **tablespoon unbleached all-purpose flour**
> 1¹/₄ **pounds white all-purpose dough, thawed if frozen**
> 2 **large bunches broccoli rabe (about 2 pounds)**
> 3 **tablespoons extra virgin olive oil**
> 3 **large cloves garlic, finely chopped**
> ¹/₄ **teaspoon red pepper flakes**
> ¹/₂ **teaspoon fennel seeds**
> **Salt and pepper to taste**
> 6 **ounces meatless sausages (about ¹/₂ package), thawed if frozen, coarsely chopped**
> 1 **tablespoon fresh lemon juice**

1. Lightly dust a 12-inch square of your counter with the flour. Place the dough on the flour and turn it over to coat lightly with flour. Cut off and discard about 4 inches of the tough bottom stems from the broccoli rabe. Cut the rabe into 2-inch pieces. Wash the rabe thoroughly in plenty of cool water to remove any grit. Drain in a colander.

2. Heat the olive oil in a large pot over low heat. Add the garlic, red pepper flakes, and fennel seeds. Cook, stirring occasionally, for 3 minutes, or until the garlic is softened but not browned. Add the broccoli rabe and sprinkle with the salt and pepper. Using tongs, turn the rabe to coat evenly with the oil. Cover and cook for 10 minutes, then turn the rabe again. Scatter the chopped sausages over the broccoli rabe, cover the pot, and continue cooking, stirring occasionally, for 20 minutes, or until the rabe is fork-tender. Stir in the lemon juice and mix well. Taste for seasonings. Turn the rabe and sausage into a colander and drain very well—if the filling is too wet, the dough will become soggy.

3. Center a rack in the oven. Preheat the oven to 375 degrees. Spray a cookie sheet with nonstick cooking spray or line it with parchment paper. Roll the dough into a 19 × 16-inch rectangle. Sprinkle the dough with a little flour if it becomes sticky as you roll it. Scatter the broccoli rabe and sausage evenly over the dough. Beginning at a long end, lift the dough over about 2 inches of the filling and roll the dough into a log shape. Pinch the ends to seal. Bend the log-shaped roll slightly to form a wide letter C. This will make it easier to transfer the roll to the cookie sheet and help it fit better on the sheet.

4. Using both hands, carefully transfer the rolled dough to the prepared cookie sheet. Cut three 1-inch slits on the top of the dough, about 3 inches apart, to allow steam to escape. Bake for 50 minutes, or until medium brown in color. Remove the bread from the oven and allow it to stand for 15 minutes, then cut into 1-inch-thick slices.

Seitan

MAKES ABOUT 4 POUNDS

Once you make homemade seitan and experience the satisfying feeling that comes from transforming two simple ingredients (flour and water) into a firm yet spongy meat that can be enjoyed in so many dishes, you'll gladly devote the five hours that you'll need from start to finish (you can get other things done while the seitan simmers for three hours). Unbleached all-purpose flour works best in this recipe. Don't use cake flour because you need the gluten in the all-purpose flour, which gives seitan a nice texture and keeps the dough from falling apart.

16 cups unbleached all-purpose flour, plus additional for kneading
6 cups cold water

Beef-Flavored Broth:

16 cups water
1 large sweet onion, coarsely chopped
2 large carrots, unpeeled, coarsely chopped
1/4 cup A-1 steak sauce
1/4 cup red wine
2 tablespoons fresh rosemary leaves or 1 tablespoon dried
6 whole black peppercorns
2 bay leaves
Salt and pepper to taste

Chicken-Flavored Broth:

16 cups water
2 large carrots, coarsely chopped
2 large parsnips, coarsely chopped
3 large ribs celery, including leaves, coarsely chopped
1 large sweet onion, coarsely chopped
1/2 cup coarsely chopped flat-leaf parsley
1 tablespoon chopped fresh or 1 teaspoon dried sage
1 tablespoon chopped fresh or 1 teaspoon dried thyme
1 1/2 teaspoons chopped fresh or 1/2 teaspoon dried marjoram
2 bay leaves
6 whole black peppercorns
Salt and pepper to taste

1. Measure the flour into a huge bowl. Pour the cold water, all at once, over the flour. Stir well with a wooden spoon, scraping the bowl to incorporate the flour as you mix. When the dough becomes too stiff to mix by spoon, begin using your hands to mix the water and flour well. Begin kneading in the bowl. The dough will be quite sticky at first, but be patient and keep kneading—the dough will become less sticky after you've kneaded it for about 5 minutes. Knead the dough for 10 to 12 minutes altogether, or until it is smooth and elastic, adding a tablespoon or two of additional flour only if the dough remains sticky after 5 minutes of kneading (usually this won't be the case except on a really humid or damp day). Knead the dough for at least 10 minutes to develop the gluten in the flour, which will give your seitan a nice chewy, meaty texture.

2. Form the dough into a ball and set it in the bowl. Pour cold (not ice) water into the bowl around the dough, not directly over the dough or the water will loosen some of it. Pour in enough cold water to cover the dough completely. Leave the bowl of dough on the counter or table for 1^1/$_2$ hours to allow the gluten to rest.

3. Meanwhile, prepare the two broths. Measure the ingredients for each broth into separate stock pots. Cover and set each on the stove, but don't turn on the heat until the seitan dough has been resting in the cold water for 1 hour. Then bring each covered pot to a boil over high heat. After the broth comes to a boil (in about 20 minutes), reduce the heat to low, cover, and cook at a low boil, stirring occasionally, for 30 to 40 minutes, or until the seitan is ready to be cooked.

4. After the seitan dough has been soaking in the cold water for 1^1/$_2$ hours, set a large colander (not a mesh strainer) in the sink. Drain the seitan dough in the colander. Rinse out the large bowl and turn the seitan into it. Set the colander in the sink. Set the bowl of seitan over the colander in the sink. Using the faucet, add enough warm water to the bowl to cover the seitan. Begin kneading the seitan in the warm water. The water will look like whole milk. Knead for 2 minutes, then turn the bowl into the colander to drain. Repeat the process of kneading for 2 minutes in warm water and draining for 8 to 10 more rinses, or until the water changes in color from that of whole milk to the gray-beige color of skim milk. Don't despair when the dough seems to fall apart; keep kneading and pushing it together as you knead, and after about 15 minutes, it will come together into a firm-spongy mass. When the water is pale gray in color, after about 20 minutes of kneading and draining, that means most of the starches have been rinsed out. Knead the seitan in the colander for 2 minutes, allowing it to drain as you knead.

5. Using your hands, transfer the seitan to a cutting board. Cut the seitan into 4 lengthwise slices. Carefully lower 2 slices of seitan into each pot of simmering broth. Cover and cook at a low boil for 2 hours, using a big spoon to turn the seitan every 30 minutes to cook evenly. Don't let the broth boil rapidly or the seitan will be tough.

6. After 2 hours the seitan will be cooked. Test by cutting with a spoon—it should cut in half easily. Turn the heat off and transfer the seitan to 2 separate plates. Reserve the broth for a soup. You can either freeze the seitan for later use or refrigerate it for up to 3 days before using it in a recipe.

Seitan Milanese

SERVES 4

The Milanese style requires that you dip the meat or vegetable into beaten eggs, then into bread crumbs, and then sauté it in heated olive oil. In this recipe we will use the meaty-textured, protein-packed, and fat-free seitan.

Note: You can make seitan at home (page 203) or you can buy it already prepared in any health foods store. I like to keep several packs in my freezer for convenience. I use White Wave brand because the slices are big, convenient for cutlets.

1 (8-ounce) package seitan, drained and cut into $1/8$-inch-thick slices
2 eggs or equivalent egg substitute
$1/4$ cup finely chopped flat-leaf parsley
  Salt and pepper to taste
1 cup plain dry bread crumbs
3 tablespoons olive oil
1 lemon, cut into wedges

1. Pat the seitan slices dry with paper towels. Combine the eggs, parsley, salt, and pepper in a shallow bowl. Beat to combine with a fork or whisk. Measure the bread crumbs into a separate shallow bowl.

2. Dip each slice of seitan first in the beaten eggs, turning to coat evenly, then in the bread crumbs, turning to coat evenly. Set the breaded slices on a platter.

3. Heat the oil in a large nonstick skillet over medium-high heat. Arrange the seitan slices in the heated oil. Cook for 3 to 4 minutes, or until medium brown, then turn and cook the other side for about 2 to 3 minutes, or until browned. Transfer to a serving platter. Serve with lemon wedges.

Seitan Francese

SERVES 4

Seitan is a protein-packed wheat meat with a meaty texture, and it's fat free! You can make your own (page 203) or you can buy it in any health foods store. Both at home and in my restaurant, I use it as a substitute for any meat. Francese means French, and in the Francese style you cook the meat in a skillet, then use the same skillet to prepare a luscious sauce of butter, lemon, and wine that is poured over the cooked meat. This is an elegant entree.

   1 **(8-ounce) package seitan, drained and cut into $1/8$-inch-thick slices**
$1/2$ **cup unbleached all-purpose flour**
     Salt and pepper to taste
   2 **eggs or equivalent egg substitute**
$1/4$ **cup finely chopped flat-leaf parsley**
$1/4$ **cup olive oil**
   1 **large clove garlic, minced**
$1/4$ **cup dry white wine**
   3 **tablespoons fresh lemon juice (about 1 lemon)**
   2 **tablespoons butter or soybean margarine**

1. Pat the slices of seitan with paper towels to dry. Measure the flour into a shallow bowl and add salt and pepper. Whisk to combine. Combine the eggs and parsley in another shallow bowl and add salt and pepper. Beat to blend with a fork or a whisk. Dredge the seitan slices in the seasoned flour, turning to coat evenly.

2. Heat the oil in a large nonstick skillet over medium heat. Add the garlic. Working quickly, dip the floured seitan slices in the egg mixture, turning to coat evenly. Arrange the slices in the heated oil. Cook for about 4 minutes, or until golden brown. Turn and cook the other side for 2 to 3 minutes, or until golden brown. Transfer to a platter.

3. Using the same skillet, combine the wine and lemon juice and add salt and pepper. Cook for 2 minutes, stirring occasionally. Add the butter and stir for about 1 minute, or until the butter melts. Taste for seasonings. Pour this sauce evenly over the seitan slices. Serve immediately.

Seitan Scarpariello

SERVES 6

This recipe is for a vegetarian dish that I make with meatless sausages, peperoncini (pickled little peppers), mushrooms, and Marsala wine. The combination of spicy sausages, Marsala, and vinegary peperoncini is luscious. Serve this stew with Roasted-Garlic Mashed Potatoes (page 30) and Sautéed Spinach (page 54) for a memorable dinner.

  1 **(8-ounce) package seitan**
  2 **tablespoons unbleached all-purpose flour**
  2 **tablespoons extra virgin olive oil**
  2 **tablespoons butter or soybean margarine**
  1 **medium yellow onion, cut into thick ribs**
  3 **large cloves garlic, cut into thick slices**
  1 **(11-ounce) package Italian-style meatless sausages, cut into 1-inch pieces**
  1 **pound large mushrooms, quartered**
      Salt and pepper to taste
12 **peperoncini, drained**
  1 **cup sweet Marsala wine**

1. Drain the seitan in a colander set in a bowl. Reserve the liquid. Cut the seitan into 1/2-inch-thick slices. Place in a bowl, sprinkle with flour, and toss to coat.

2. Heat the olive oil and butter in a large deep skillet, over medium heat. Add the onion, garlic, sausages, mushrooms, salt, and pepper. Cover and cook, stirring occasionally, for 20 minutes, or until the onion is soft and the mushrooms have released their moisture. Add the peperoncini and the flour-coated seitan. Stir well to mix. Cover and cook for 3 minutes, stirring occasionally.

3. Add the reserved liquid from the seitan and the Marsala. Continue cooking, uncovered, stirring frequently, for 15 minutes, or until the mixture has thickened and is reduced by about one-half. Taste for seasonings.

Fava Beans and Smothered Onions over Seitan

SERVES 6

Fava beans are very large, flat beans with a mild flavor and creamy texture. The skins on dried fava beans can be tough, so even after cooking, most people remove them. You can either blanch the beans, slip off the skins, and then cook the beans, or as in this recipe, you can cook the beans and then remove the skins.

Note: Seitan is an ancient Asian staple known as wheat meat. It is rich in protein, fat free, and has a wonderful meaty texture. You can make your own (page 203) or buy it already prepared in the refrigerated section of health foods stores.

> 1 **pound dried fava beans, picked over for stones**
> $1/4$ **cup unbleached all-purpose flour**
> 1 **(8-ounce) package seitan, drained and cut into thin cutlets**
> **Salt and pepper to taste**
> 4 **cloves garlic, coarsely chopped**
> 3 **tablespoons extra virgin olive oil**
> 4 **large yellow onions, cut into thick ribs, separated**

1. Place the dried fava beans and 3 quarts of water in a large covered pot over high heat. Bring to a boil and cook for about 1 hour, or until the beans are fork-tender. Drain. Return the beans to the pot and cover them with cold water. When cool enough to handle, slip off the skins. Set the skinned beans aside.

2. Measure the flour into a shallow bowl. Dredge the seitan cutlets in the flour, turning to coat both sides. Shake off the excess. Sprinkle both sides with salt and pepper.

3. Spray a large nonstick skillet with olive oil cooking spray. Heat the skillet over medium-high heat. Add half of the chopped garlic and the floured seitan cutlets. Cook each side for 1 to 2 minutes, or until medium brown, then turn and brown the other side for about 1 minute, or until medium brown. Transfer the browned cutlets to a platter.

4. Heat the olive oil in the same nonstick skillet over medium heat. Add the remaining chopped garlic, the onions, salt, and pepper. Cover and cook, stirring occasionally, for 10 to 12 minutes, or until the onions are soft and golden brown. Taste for seasonings. Arrange the fava beans evenly over the seitan cutlets. Turn the cooked onions onto the fava beans, using a rubber spatula to scrape the juices out of the skillet. Serve immediately.

Desserts

Sweet Crespelle (Sweet Crepes)
Chocolate-Covered Eggplant
Easter Sweet Bread
Barley Pie
Pignoli Cookies
Fried Struffoli
Baked Struffoli
Sweet Ricotta
Italian Rice Pudding
Sponge Cake
Chocolate and Almond Stuffed Figs
Italian Fruit Salad
Cherries in Vermouth
Ice Box Cake
Zabaglione
Italian Cream
Cream Puffs
Anginettes
Apples Baked with Sugar, Lemon, and White Wine
Anisette Dunking Cookies
Anisette Glaze

Sweet Crespelle (Sweet Crepes)

MAKES 12

In the heart of Amalfi, I enjoyed unforgettable crespelle made with a thin layer of Nutella, a chocolate-hazelnut spread, which melts ever so slightly into the crepe. Once the Nutella is spread on a warm crepe, it is folded in half and then in half again, and the top is dusted lightly with confectioners sugar mixed with cocoa powder. These are amazingly tender and luscious triangles of pure pleasure. You can also serve them with apricot or strawberry jam or a combination of Nutella and apricot jam.

- 2 **cups unbleached all-purpose flour**
- 1/4 **cup sugar**
- 4 **eggs or 1 cup egg substitute**
- 1 **teaspoon vanilla extract**
- 2 **cups water**
- 3/4 **cup Nutella and/or apricot or strawberry jam**
- 1/4 **cup confectioners sugar**
- 2 **tablespoons cocoa powder**

1. Measure the flour and sugar into a large bowl. Stir to combine. In a separate bowl, combine the eggs, vanilla, and water. Whisk well to blend. Pour the liquid mixture over the flour mixture all at once, using a rubber spatula to scrape out the bowl. Whisk the mixture together until well blended. It should have the consistency of pancake batter.

2. Line a cookie sheet with wax paper and set it by the stove. Spray a large nonstick skillet with nonstick cooking spray. Heat it over medium heat. Pour 1/3 cup of the batter into the center of the heated skillet, then quickly tilt the skillet to spread the batter and coat the entire bottom of the skillet. Cook for 1 to 2 minutes, or until the crepe looks set and the underside is golden brown. Turn the crepe over and cook the other side for a minute or two, or until golden brown. Transfer the crepe to the lined cookie sheet and begin another crepe.

3. While the next crepe is cooking, spread a tablespoon of the Nutella or jam evenly over the cooked one while it is still warm. Fold the crepe in half and then in half again, forming a triangle. Continue cooking and filling and folding the crepes. Place the confectioners sugar and cocoa in a sifter and dust the tops of the crepes.

Chocolate~Covered Eggplant

SERVES 6

For as long as I can remember, my mom's childhood friend Teresa Amendola has made this special dessert for my mom on the Assumption of Mary. This date, August 15, is my grandmother's name day, and name days along with patron saint days are always a special occasion in Italian communities. While chocolate with eggplant may sound a bit odd, I promise that everyone who has ever tasted this dessert was impressed by its unique and tantalizing flavor.

    1 **cup golden raisins**
1/4 **cup gin**
    2 **medium eggplants**
1/4 **to** 1/2 **cup canola oil**
1/2 **cup unbleached all-purpose flour**
    3 **eggs**
    6 **ounces unsweetened chocolate, cut into small pieces**
1/2 **cup sugar**
1/4 **teaspoon ground cinnamon**
1/4 **cup candied citron, finely chopped**
1/2 **cup pine nuts**

1. Place the raisins in a bowl, add the gin, and stir to mix. Set aside to plump. Line a platter with a double layer of paper towels and set it by the stove. Peel the eggplant and cut it into 1/4-inch-thick rounds.

2. Heat 2 tablespoons of the oil in a large nonstick skillet over medium heat. Place as many slices of eggplant as you can fit in the skillet. Cook for about 2 minutes, or until softened, then turn and cook the other side for 1 to 2 minutes, or until softened. Transfer to the towel-lined platter. Continue frying the remaining eggplant slices, heating additional oil as needed.

3. Clean the skillet and set it on the stove. Measure the flour into a shallow bowl. Whisk the eggs in a separate bowl.

4. Heat 2 tablespoons of the oil in the clean skillet over medium heat. Working quickly, dredge the eggplant slices, one at a time, first in the flour, turning to coat evenly, then in the beaten eggs, turning to coat. Place the coated eggplant in the skillet, fitting as many as you can without crowding. Cook each side until golden brown, about 2 minutes per side. Transfer to the towel-lined platter.

5. Melt the chocolate in the top of a double boiler over simmering water. Whisk in the sugar and cinnamon. Taste and add an additional tablespoon or two of sugar, if desired.

6. While the chocolate is melting, drain the raisins and place in a bowl. Add the citron and pine nuts. Stir to mix.

7. Set out a large round plate and a large platter. Spread a little melted chocolate in a 3-inch circle on the round plate. Place an eggplant cutlet on the chocolate and move the eggplant in the chocolate to coat. Transfer the coated eggplant slice to the platter. Spoon a little chocolate over the eggplant. Spoon a heaping teaspoon of the raisin filling in the center of the eggplant. Drizzle chocolate over the filling. Top the filling with another eggplant slice. Spoon a little chocolate over the top and spread the chocolate to coat the eggplant.

7. Repeat this process with the remaining eggplant slices. When you have finished, cover the platter with wax paper and chill before eating.

Easter Sweet Bread

MAKES A 10-INCH BUNDT LOAF

My Aunt Rose makes this traditional Italian sweet bread every Easter, and now I make it at home and in my restaurant. Serve it with a cup of espresso or a glass of milk. Leftovers will keep for several days, so enjoy them on your afternoon coffee break.

$1/2$ **cup milk**
8 **ounces butter (2 sticks), cut into several pieces**
5 **eggs**
2 **teaspoons lemon extract**
1 **cup sugar**
$1/2$ **teaspoon salt**
  Grated zest of 1 orange
$1/2$ **cup fresh orange juice (about 1 orange)**
$1/4$ **cup warm tap water**
1 **tablespoon active dry yeast**
5 **cups unbleached all-purpose flour**
1 **teaspoon baking powder**

1. Heat the milk and butter in a pot over medium heat until the butter melts and the milk scalds. Turn into a large bowl. Set aside for about 20 minutes to cool slightly.

2. Using a whisk, beat the eggs, lemon extract, sugar, salt, orange zest, and juice into the milk mixture.

3. Measure the warm water into a bowl. Sprinkle the yeast over the water, stir briefly to mix, and set aside to proof for about 10 minutes, or until it foams. In a separate bowl, combine the flour and baking powder. Stir to mix.

4. After the yeast has proofed, add it to the liquid mixture and beat well with a whisk. Add the flour mixture all at once and beat with a spoon.

5. Preheat the oven to 325 degrees. Spray a 10-inch tube pan with nonstick cooking spray. Turn the batter into the prepared pan, using a rubber spatula to scrape out the bowl and to smooth the top of the batter. Bake for 1 hour, or until the top is golden brown and a cake tester inserted into the center comes out clean. Turn out to cool slightly before cutting. If desired, drizzle with Anisette Glaze (page 238).

Barley Pie

SERVES 8

Every Easter my Aunts Rose, Marge, and Connie would bring their barley pies to my grandparents' house for Grandpa's approval. Luckily, they arrived separately, because after tasting each of their pies, Grandpa would proclaim it to be the best. I have combined the three recipes into this one.

Sweet Crust:
>   2   cups unbleached all-purpose flour
> $1/2$ cup sugar
> $1/8$ teaspoon salt
>   2   tablespoons baking powder
> $1/4$ cup butter or soybean margarine ($1/2$ stick), cut into small pieces
>   2   egg yolks
> $1/4$ cup plus 2 tablespoons milk or soy milk

Filling:
>   2   quarts milk or soy milk
>   1   pound barley
> $1/2$ cup sugar
>   1   tablespoon grated lemon zest
>   1   pound ricotta cheese
>   7   eggs
>   1   teaspoon vanilla extract
>   1   tablespoon fresh lemon juice (about $1/2$ lemon)

1. To prepare the sweet crust, measure the flour, sugar, salt, and baking powder into a bowl. Sift this into another bowl. With a pastry blender or 2 knives, cut the butter into the dry mixture until the mixture resembles coarse meal.

2. Whisk the egg yolks and milk in a bowl. Pour this over the flour mixture, using a rubber spatula to scrape out the bowl. Stir to combine into a dough.

3. Lightly dust the counter with flour. Turn the dough out onto the floured area and knead for about 2 minutes, or until smooth. Cut the dough in half, wrap each half in plastic or wax paper, and refrigerate for 1 hour to chill.

4. To make the filling, combine the milk and barley in a large, heavy pot. Cook over medium heat, stirring occasionally, for about 1 hour, or until the barley is tender and the milk is absorbed. If the barley begins to stick, lower the heat to medium-low.

5. Remove from the heat and stir in the sugar, lemon zest, ricotta, 6 of the eggs, the vanilla, and the lemon juice. Beat with a spoon to combine.

6. Preheat the oven to 350 degrees. Spray a 10-inch deep-dish pie pan with nonstick cooking spray. Lightly dust the counter with flour. Remove the dough from the refrigerator and unwrap it. Roll out one dough half into a 14-inch round. Fit the dough into the prepared pie pan, overlapping the edges. Roll out the other half of the dough into a 12-inch round. Cut the dough into 17 or 18 half-inch strips.

7. Pour the filling into the pie pan, using a rubber spatula to scrape the pot of the filling and to smooth the top. (If you have extra filling, bake it in a custard cup for 1 hour, or until set.) Arrange the dough strips in a crisscross pattern over the filling. Cut the edges of dough, then press the strips and the bottom crust together. Crimp the edges with your fingers.

8. Place the remaining egg yolk in a bowl and beat it with a fork to blend. Brush the yolk over the strips. Sprinkle a little sugar evenly over the top. Place the pie on a cookie sheet and bake for about 1 hour, or until the top is golden brown.

Pignoli Cookies

MAKES ABOUT 34 COOKIES

Pignoli are the most popular cookie in my family, and they are also the most expensive to make because pine nuts and almond paste (the main ingredients) cost a small fortune. They are, however, a special treat for Christmas, at weddings, and at bridal showers, where it is customary to give the guests cookies to take home.

14 **ounces almond paste**
1 **cup sugar**
1/2 **cup unbleached all-purpose flour**
3 **egg whites**
8 **ounces pine nuts (about 1 3/4 cups)**

1. Center the oven racks. Preheat the oven to 325 degrees. Spray 2 cookie sheets with nonstick cooking spray.

2. Place the almond paste, sugar, and flour in a large bowl. Using a hand mixer, beat the ingredients on medium speed for 2 to 3 minutes, or until the mixture is in large crumbs. Using your fingers, rub the mixture until the crumbs are fine (this will take about 10 minutes).

3. In a separate bowl, beat the egg whites on medium speed for about 4 minutes, or until soft peaks form. Using a rubber spatula, gently but thoroughly fold the beaten egg whites into the almond paste mixture. Gently stir 1/4 cup of the pine nuts into the mixture.

4. Place the remaining pine nuts in a shallow bowl. For each cookie, form a rounded teaspoon of dough into a 1- to 1 1/2-inch log, then carefully roll the log into the pine nuts to coat. Shape each cookie into a crescent shape.

5. Arrange the cookies on the prepared cookie sheets, leaving about 1 inch of space in between them. Bake for about 18 minutes, or until golden brown, rotating the cookie sheets after about 14 minutes so the bottoms will bake evenly. Carefully remove the cookies to a platter. They will become firm and less fragile as they cool. After they cool to room temperature, store for up to 1 week in a tightly covered tin.

Fried Struffoli

MAKES ABOUT 250 LITTLE BALLS

Struffoli are little nuggets of sweetened dough coated with honey. This is another special Christmas and Easter Sunday treat in the Italian American family.

> 9 **cups unbleached all-purpose flour**
> 6 **tablespoons sugar**
> 4 **teaspoons baking powder**
> $1/4$ **teaspoon salt**
> 10 **eggs**
> $1/2$ **cup corn or canola oil**
> 3 **tablespoons vanilla extract**
> 5 **cups canola oil**
> 2 **cups honey**

1. Measure the flour, sugar, baking powder, and salt into a large bowl. Stir well to mix.

2. In a separate bowl, whisk together the eggs, corn oil, and vanilla until blended. Pour the liquid mixture over the flour mixture all at once. Stir well to mix. Knead the mixture in the bowl until it holds together, about 2 minutes, then turn out onto a counter and knead for about 5 minutes, or until smooth.

3. Roll the dough into a thick log shape about 14 inches long. Cut into 1-inch-thick slices. Roll each slice into a rope shape about 14 inches long. Cut each rope into $1/2$-inch pieces. Roll each piece into a little ball.

4. Heat the canola oil in a large pot over medium-high heat. Line 2 cookie sheets or a large deep roasting pan with brown paper bags or a triple layer of paper towels and set by the stove. Drop 18 to 20 little balls into the hot oil. Cook, stirring occasionally, for 2 to 3 minutes, or until golden brown. Using a slotted spoon or strainer, transfer the struffoli to the paper-lined cookie sheets. After you have fried all the struffoli, transfer them to a large bowl.

5. Heat the honey in a small pot over low heat. Drizzle the heated honey over the struffoli, and toss the balls to coat evenly. After the struffoli cool to room temperature, store in a tightly covered container for up to 1 week.

Baked Struffoli

MAKES ABOUT 160 LITTLE COOKIES

Baked struffoli are a delicious and satisfying alternative to the fried version.

8 cups unbleached all-purpose flour
1 tablespoon baking powder
1/2 cup sugar
1/4 teaspoon salt
8 eggs
1 cup corn or canola oil
1 tablespoon vanilla extract
2 cups honey

1. Preheat the oven to 350 degrees. Spray 2 to 4 cookie sheets with nonstick cooking spray.

2. Combine the flour, baking powder, sugar, and salt in a large bowl. Stir well to mix. In a separate bowl, combine the eggs, oil, and vanilla. Whisk well to blend. Pour the egg mixture over the flour mixture. Stir well to mix.

3. Turn the dough out onto a countertop. Knead until the dough is smooth, 5 to 6 minutes. Roll the dough into a 14-inch-long log. Cut off a 2-inch-thick slice. Roll the slice into a 17-inch-long rope. Cut the rope into 1/2-inch-long pieces. Arrange the pieces on the prepared cookie sheets, leaving 1/2 inch of space between them. Repeat the process with the remaining dough. Bake the struffoli for about 15 minutes, or until golden brown.

4. Meanwhile, heat the honey in a small saucepan over low heat. Turn the baked struffoli into a large bowl. While the struffoli are still warm, drizzle them with about 1/4 cup of heated honey for every 2 or 3 trays of cookies. Toss well to coat the cookies. Let cool to room temperature, then store in a tightly covered container.

Sweet Ricotta

MAKES 2 CUPS

This dessert is delicious when served alone in a pretty dessert dish or when topped with Cherries in Vermouth (page 229). It also makes a luscious topping for Sponge Cake (page 225) or Cream Puffs (page 233). My mom would also spread Sweet Ricotta on her morning little toasts.

$^1/_4$ **cup golden raisins**
3 **tablespoons sweet vermouth**
1 **pound ricotta cheese**
$^1/_4$ **cup confectioners sugar, sifted**

Place the raisins in a cup, add the vermouth, and stir to mix. Set aside to plump for about 30 minutes, stirring occasionally. Place the ricotta cheese in a bowl. Add the sugar and the raisins with the vermouth. Stir well to combine. Serve immediately or chilled.

Italian Rice Pudding

SERVES 6

Arborio, the plump Italian risotto rice, adds a rich texture to this rice pudding. For a zesty taste, the golden raisins are plumped in gin.

$1/2$ **cup golden raisins**
   3 **tablespoons gin**
   6 **eggs**
$1/2$ **cup sugar**
   4 **cups milk or soy milk**
   1 **tablespoon vanilla extract**
   2 **teaspoons ground cinnamon**
$1/8$ **teaspoon ground nutmeg**
   4 **cups cooked Arborio rice**

1. Preheat the oven to 350 degrees. Place the raisins in a shallow bowl, add the gin, and set aside to plump.

2. Combine the eggs, sugar, milk, vanilla, cinnamon, and nutmeg in a bowl. Beat with a whisk to combine. Add the rice. Drain the raisins and add them to the bowl. Mix well.

3. Spray a 3-quart glass baking dish with nonstick cooking spray. Pour the rice pudding mixture into the dish, using a rubber spatula to scrape the bowl clean and then to smooth the mixture. Place the dish into a larger baking dish. Pour enough water into the larger dish to come halfway up the sides of the filled dish.

4. Carefully place the dish in the oven and bake for $1^1/2$ hours, or until the pudding is set. Remove from the oven and serve, or cool to room temperature and refrigerate until needed.

Sponge Cake

MAKES A 10-INCH TUBE CAKE

This is the traditional cake that my mom made for my siblings and me on our birthdays until we married. It is a wonderful dessert for special as well as casual occasions.

10 eggs, separated
1 cup sugar
2 tablespoons grated lemon zest
$1/4$ cup fresh lemon juice (about 1 lemon)
2 teaspoons vanilla extract
2 cups sifted unbleached all-purpose flour
$1/8$ teaspoon salt

Filling:
1 pint fresh strawberries, sliced
2 tablespoons sugar
1 pint heavy cream
2 tablespoons confectioners sugar

1. Center the oven rack. Preheat the oven to 325 degrees. Spray a 10-inch tube pan with nonstick cooking spray.

2. Using a hand mixer on medium speed, beat the egg yolks and sugar in a large bowl for about 5 minutes, or until the mixture is pale yellow. Add the lemon zest, lemon juice, vanilla, and flour. Mix on low speed for 1 minute, stopping once or twice to scrape the bowl with a rubber spatula.

3. In a large bowl, beat the egg whites (make sure you wash and dry the mixer blades first) with the salt for 5 to 6 minutes, or until medium-firm peaks form. Gently but thoroughly fold the beaten egg whites into the flour mixture, using a rubber spatula. Turn the cake batter into the prepared tube pan, using a rubber spatula to scrape out the bowl and to smooth the top. Bake for about 1 hour, or until a cake tester inserted into the center comes out clean.

4. Remove the cake from the oven. Using a long metal spatula, loosen the sides of the cake from the pan, then turn out onto a cooling rack. While the cake is cooling to room temperature, prepare the filling.

5. Place the sliced strawberries in a bowl. Sprinkle with the sugar and toss to combine. In a separate bowl, beat the cream with a hand mixer on medium-high speed until it forms soft peaks.

6. When the cake has cooled to room temperature, cut it in half horizontally. Sift the confectioners sugar evenly onto a cake plate (this will help to prevent the cake from sticking to the plate). Place the bottom layer of the cake, cut side up, on the plate. Spoon the sliced strawberries and their juices evenly onto the cake. Allow the juices to soak in for about 30 minutes. Place the top layer of cake on the bottom layer. Spread the whipped cream evenly over the cake, using a rubber spatula. Serve immediately or refrigerate for up to 1 day.

Chocolate and Almond Stuffed Figs

SERVES 8

When my mother and her girlfriends would get together for a typical Italian-style picnic, which included on the menu foods like roasted peppers, cauliflower pancakes, and polenta, they often took along stuffed figs for dessert.

16 large dried figs (Mission or other)
1 cup orange juice (preferably fresh)
1/4 cup chocolate chips
15 whole almonds

1. Cut a 1-inch-long slit in each fig, about two-thirds through. Place the cut figs in a shallow bowl, add the orange juice, and let the figs plump somewhat and absorb some of the juice for about 1 hour.

2. Preheat the oven to 350 degrees. Spray a glass baking dish large enough to accommodate the figs in a single layer with nonstick cooking spray.

3. Drain the figs, reserving the juice. Open each fig and stuff the slit with 3 or 4 chocolate chips. Top each slit with an almond.

4. Arrange the stuffed figs in a single layer in the prepared baking dish. Pour the reserved juice evenly over the figs. Cover the dish tightly with foil. Bake for 30 minutes. To serve, spoon the figs into a dish and spoon a little of the juice evenly over the top.

Italian Fruit Salad

SERVES 6

My mom often squeezes fresh lemon juice onto a slice of honeydew or cantaloupe and onto most other fruits as well, but it was not until I ate the fruit salads in Amalfi that I realized the connection between my mother's love of lemons (she buys them by the dozen) and her family ties to Italian cuisine. The entire coast, from the bay of Naples to Salerno, is studded with beautiful lemon trees growing along the mountainside in tiered gardens.

Note: Use the best fruit available; any variety will be delicious.

> 2 ripe pears, cored and cut into bite-size pieces
> 2 apples, cored and cut into bite-size pieces
> 2 ripe peaches, peeled, pitted, and cut into bite-size pieces
> 2 ripe plums, pitted and cut into bite-size pieces
> 2 ripe bananas, cut into 1-inch-thick slices
> 1/4 cup sugar
> 6 tablespoons fresh lemon juice (about 2 lemons)
> 2 tablespoons dry white wine

Place the cut fruit in a bowl and toss gently to combine. Sprinkle the sugar, lemon juice, and wine evenly over the fruit. Toss gently but thoroughly to combine.

Cherries in Vermouth

SERVES 6

Every summer my grandparents packed big jars with plump cherries and covered them with vermouth for a refreshing treat that lasted longer than for one occasion. Cherries in Vermouth tastes fabulous on its own and makes an ideal topping spooned over Sponge Cake (page 225) or sweetened ricotta cheese (1 pound ricotta cheese with 3 tablespoons confectioners sugar, sifted).

30 **large cherries, stemmed**
 1 **tablespoon sugar**
 1 **cup sweet vermouth**

Place the cherries in a bowl and sprinkle with the sugar. Toss to coat. Turn into a wide-mouthed jar with a tight-fitting cap. Pour the vermouth over the cherries and stir to mix. Keep the cherries covered with vermouth. Allow to marinate for at least a day. They will keep unrefrigerated, for up to a month.

Ice Box Cake

SERVES 8

This rich dessert of graham crackers layered with chocolate and vanilla Italian Cream is so addictive that we had to stop making it at Claire's. Many of us found it just too irresistible and ate it every day, wreaking havoc on both our food costs and our waists. Many customers still request this old Italian favorite, so we do occasionally make it.

> **6 cups Italian Cream (page 232)**
> **$1/4$ cup cocoa powder, sifted**
> **23 whole graham crackers**
> **3 ripe bananas, thinly sliced**

1. Spoon 2 cups of the Italian cream into a bowl. Add the sifted cocoa powder. Stir well to mix.

2. Line the bottom of a 13 x 9-inch glass baking dish with a layer of graham crackers, breaking them to fit. Spoon the chocolate Italian Cream over the graham crackers, using the back of the spoon to smooth the top. Arrange one-third of the banana slices evenly over the cream. Arrange another layer of graham crackers over the bananas. Spoon half of the plain Italian cream over the crackers, smoothing the top. Arrange one-third of the banana slices over the cream. Repeat the layers, ending with banana slices on top. Crumble a graham cracker in your hands and sprinkle evenly over the banana slices.

3. Cover the pan with plastic wrap and refrigerate until well chilled. The graham crackers will soften as they absorb the Italian cream. Cut into squares and serve.

Zabaglione

SERVES 6

Zabaglione (pronounced za-bal-YO-nay) is one of the richest yet surprisingly light traditional Italian desserts. It's a delectable mixture of egg yolks, sugar, and Marsala wine whisked over simmering water until it becomes light and foamy. I like to spoon it over plump ripe strawberries in a wine glass and eat it while it's still warm. It is equally elegant served plain or chilled.

12 large ripe strawberries, cut in half
5 egg yolks
1 whole egg
1/2 cup plus 2 tablespoons sugar
1 cup Marsala wine

1. Divide the strawberries among 6 wine glasses. Place a metal bowl over a large pot of water to make sure the bowl fits securely and the bottom doesn't touch the water. Remove the bowl and bring the water to a simmer over medium heat.

2. Place the egg yolks, whole egg, and sugar in the bowl. Whisk together until pale yellow and well blended. Place the bowl over the simmering water. Whisk continuously for about 10 minutes, or until the mixture coats the back of a spoon.

3. Add the Marsala and whisk continuously for about 10 minutes, or until the mixture is the consistency of thin pastry cream and has increased in volume by more than double. Pour the zabaglione over the strawberries in the wine glasses. Stir to mix. Serve immediately or chilled.

Italian Cream

MAKES ABOUT 8 CUPS

This rich traditional Italian cream makes a great filling for Cream Puffs (page 233) and for Ice Box Cake (page 230). By itself, is a perfect pudding.

8 egg yolks
1 cup sugar
2¹/₂ cups unbleached all-purpose flour
6¹/₂ cups whole milk
1 tablespoon cornstarch
1 tablespoon finely grated lemon zest
1 tablespoon finely grated orange zest
2 teaspoons vanilla extract

1. Place the egg yolks and sugar in a bowl. Beat with a wooden spoon for about 1 minute, or until pale and light. Add the flour. Beat well for 2 to 3 minutes, or until well combined and crumbly. Slowly add the milk, whisking continuously until the mixture is well blended. Add the cornstarch, whisking until well blended.

2. Pour the mixture into a large, heavy pot, using a rubber spatula to scrape out the bowl. Bring to a low boil, stirring constantly, over low-medium heat (this will take 35 to 40 minutes). The mixture will become thick and creamy. Remove from the heat.

3. Stir in the lemon and orange zest and vanilla, whisking until well blended. Turn into a bowl. Cover with wax paper, pressing the paper onto the surface of the hot cream to prevent a skin from forming. Let cool to room temperature before using for ice box cake, or refrigerate overnight before filling cream puffs.

Cream Puffs

MAKES 14 CREAM PUFFS

When I was growing up, my mom made these cream puffs every Saturday. They are delicious plain, with just a dusting of confectioners sugar, or drizzled with melted chocolate. After they are cooled from baking, the puffs can be sliced in half horizontally and filled with either unsweetened whipped cream or with Italian Cream (page 232). If you choose to fill the puffs with a variety of fillings, try adding chocolate.

1 **cup water**
$^1/_2$ **cup butter (1 stick) or vegetable shortening**
$^1/_8$ **teaspoon salt**
1 **cup unbleached all-purpose flour**
4 **eggs**

1. Center the oven racks. Preheat the oven to 400 degrees.

2. Bring the water, butter, and salt to a rapid boil over high heat. Stir frequently until the butter melts. Add the flour all at once and beat with a wooden spoon. Cook for 1 to 2 minutes, beating continuously. The mixture will pull away from the sides of the pan. Turn off the heat and remove the pan from the heat. Continue beating for 1 minute to allow the mixture to cool slightly.

3. Add the eggs, one at a time, beating well for about 45 seconds before adding the next egg. The mixture will look lumpy and separated somewhat, but keep beating vigorously until it is smooth and glossy, about 45 seconds after adding the last egg.

4. Drop heaping tablespoons of batter onto ungreased cookie sheets, leaving about 2 inches of space between them to allow for rising. Bake for 25 minutes. Rotate the cookie sheets from top to bottom and front to back, and continue baking for an additional 20 to 25 minutes, or until the cream puffs are golden brown and firm to the touch. Allow to cool to room temperature before filling if desired.

Anginettes

MAKES ABOUT 10 DOZEN

Anginettes are delicious cookies that were always present on major occasions at our house. You'll find them at traditional Italian bridal showers, weddings, and christenings, as well as at Christmas and Easter celebrations. They keep well in a covered tin, but don't expect them to last, especially if your family takes to them as much as mine has.

1	pound butter, softened to room temperature
3$^{1}/_{2}$	cups sugar
6	eggs
4	teaspoons vanilla extract
2	pounds ricotta cheese
8	cups unbleached all-purpose flour
2	teaspoons baking powder
2	teaspoons baking soda
2	teaspoons salt

Glaze:

2$^{1}/_{2}$	cups confectioners sugar
3	tablespoons orange juice
2	tablespoons milk or soy milk

1. Place the softened butter in a large bowl. Beat until smooth, using a hand mixer on low speed. Add the sugar. Beat well on medium speed for about 3 minutes, or until well blended, stopping once or twice to scrape down the sides of the bowl with a rubber spatula. Add the eggs, 2 at a time, beating on low speed for 1 minute after each addition. Add the vanilla and the ricotta. Mix on low speed for 1 to 2 minutes, or until blended.

2. Preheat the oven to 350 degrees. Measure the flour, baking powder, soda, and salt into a bowl. Stir to combine. Add this all at once to the creamed mixture. Using a wooden spoon, stir until all of the flour is mixed into the creamed mixture. The batter should be fairly stiff.

3. Drop teaspoons of batter onto ungreased cookie sheets, leaving about 1$^{1}/_{2}$ inches of space in between the cookies to allow for spreading. Bake for about 10 minutes. rotating the cookie sheets from top to bottom and front to back, and continue baking for another 10 minutes, or until the cookies are golden brown and firm to the touch. Let cool to room temperature before glazing.

4. To make the glaze, sift the confectioners sugar into a small bowl. Add the orange juice and milk and beat until soft and creamy. Drizzle evenly over the cooled anginettes.

Apples Baked with Sugar, Lemon, and White Wine

SERVES 6

Now that a beautiful selection of apples is available year-round, you can enjoy this fat-free Italian counterpart to apple brown betty every season. I like to use organic Fuji apples, but this recipe is delicious even with the old standby, McIntosh, which is what my grandmother always used.

> **6** **large apples, cored and cut into $1/2$-inch-thick slices**
> **6** **tablespoons fresh lemon juice (about 2 lemons)**
> **6** **tablespoons dry white wine**
> **$1/2$** **cup sugar**
> **1** **cup plain dry bread crumbs**

1. Preheat the oven to 375 degrees. Place the sliced apples in a large bowl. Add the lemon juice and wine and toss well to coat. Add the sugar and bread crumbs. Toss well to coat.

2. Spray a 13 × 9-inch glass baking dish with butter-flavored cooking spray. Turn the apple mixture into the prepared baking dish, using a rubber spatula to scrape the bowl of any juices. Cover tightly with foil. Bake for 1 hour 15 minutes, or until the apples are tender when tested with a fork.

Anisette Dunking Cookies

MAKES ABOUT 44 COOKIES

My grandmother always had a plate of these anise-flavored cookies on hand for dunking into a cup of espresso or a glass of milk. After they are baked and cooled to room temperature, drizzle them with Anisette Glaze (page 238) and start dunking!

- 4 cups unbleached all-purpose flour
- 5 teaspoons baking powder
- 1/4 teaspoon salt
- 1 cup sugar
- 2 eggs
- 3/4 cup milk or soy milk
- 1/2 cup canola oil
- 3 tablespoons anisette liqueur or Sambuca

1. Preheat the oven to 375 degrees. Measure the flour, baking powder, salt, and sugar into a bowl. Sift this into another bowl. In a separate bowl, combine the eggs, milk, oil, and anisette. Whisk to blend well. Pour this over the dry ingredients, using a rubber spatula to scrape out the bowl. Stir the mixture to combine. The batter will be thick.

2. Spray 2 or 3 cookie sheets with nonstick cooking spray. Drop heaping teaspoons of batter onto the cookie sheets, leaving 1 1/2 inches of space between them. Bake for about 12 minutes, or until golden brown. Transfer the cookies to a platter to cool before drizzling with a glaze or storing.

Anisette Glaze

MAKES ABOUT 1 CUP

This glaze is perfect for drizzling over Anisette Dunking Cookies (page 237) or Sponge Cake (page 225), as well as many other cookies and cakes.

2 cups confectioners sugar, sifted
2 tablespoons anisette liqueur
2 tablespoons milk or soy milk

Combine the ingredients in a bowl. Stir until smooth and creamy. Use immediately.

Index

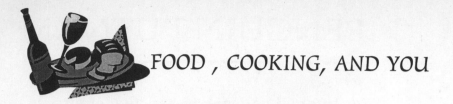 FOOD , COOKING, AND YOU

FROM PENGUIN PUTNAM INC.

☐**THE ALL-IN-ONE DIABETIC COOKBOOK**
   by P.J. Palumbo, M.D. and Joyce Daly Margie
                              0-452-26467-7/$13.95

☐**THE CARBOHYDRATE ADDICT'S LIFESPAN PROGRAM**
   by Dr. Richard Heller and Dr. Rachael Heller
                              0-452-27838-4/$14.95

☐**THE SOY GOURMET** by Robin Robertson
                              0-452-27922-4/$11.95

☐**366 DELICIOUS WAYS TO COOK PASTA WITH VEGETABLES**
   by Dolores Riccio   0-452-27727-2/$16.95

☐**CLAIRE'S CORNER COPIA COOKBOOK** by Claire Criscuolo
                              0-452-27176-2/$14.95

Prices slightly higher in Canada.